SOMEBODY ELSE'S CHILDREN

SOMEBODY ELSE'S CHILDREN

Sally Trench

Hodder & Stoughton
LONDON SYDNEY AUCKLAND TORONTO

This story is fact: for obvious reasons, names, places
and dates have been changed

British Library Cataloguing in Publication Data
Trench, Sally
  Somebody else's children.
  1. Great Britain. Maladjusted children. Education
  I. Title
  371.93

ISBN 0-340-53492-3

Published by Hodder and Stoughton,
a division of Hodder and Stoughton Ltd,
Mill Road, Dunton Green, Sevenoaks, Kent TN13 2YA
Editorial Office: 47 Bedford Square, London WC1B 3DP

Typeset by Hewer Text Composition Services, Edinburgh
Printed in Great Britain by Clays Ltd, St. Ives plc

It is a fact of life that one can choose one's friends but not one's family. For this reason I dedicate this book to Christopher and Nicholas, who had no choice!

Abou Ben Adhem

Abou Ben Adhem (may his tribe increase!)
Awoke one night from a deep dream of peace,
And saw, within the moonlight in his room,
Making it rich, and like a lily in bloom,
An angel writing in a book of gold:–
Exceeding peace had made Ben Adhem bold,
And to the presence in the room he said,
  'What writest thou?' – The vision raised its head,
And with a look of sweet accord,
Answered, 'The names of those that love the Lord.'
  'And is mine one?' said Abou. 'Nay, not so,'
Replied the angel. Abou spoke more low,
But cheerly still; and said, 'I pray thee, then,
Write me as one that loves his fellow men.'
  The angel wrote, and vanished. The next night
It came again with a great wakening light,
And showed the names whom love of God had blest,
And lo! Ben Adhem's name led all the rest.

James Leigh Hunt
(1784–1859)

Introduction

In the 1960s, as a teenager, I wrote the first lines of my first book, *Bury Me In My Boots*, on toilet paper in Waterloo Station. It became a best-seller. For me it was an unbelievable fluke. I was compared with St Joan of Arc and invited for cocktails at Buckingham Palace. I never really understood why, for the compassion and care I gave in my daily work on the London streets among drug-addicts and alcoholics was as instinctive to me as it was for a priest to say mass. I am not a religious extremist; if I had been, I should have left the sorrows and troubles of human suffering, in their unnecessary abundance, to His immortal compass. Nor am I by nature a do-gooder. I believe I am a person born in complete disagreement with the spirit of the age, who has been privileged to offer a way of life that gives hope to the young, inspiration to the disadvantaged and compassion to the delinquent.

This book is the true story of how young teenagers grew up to find their birthright, through old-fashioned qualities of love, respect and discipline. This book is not a fluke. I wrote it because I needed to share my extraordinary experiences not only with parents and teachers, but with a world that appears to be becoming stunted by the daily miseries of a materialistically motivated society. Like reality, this book is full of pathos, humour, disappointment, success. Above all, it is the story of faith and hope invested in an almost spiritually bankrupt society, which has no vision to grasp the roots of its problems, and spares little time and even less commitment to identify its symptoms.

Sally Trench
November 1989

Chapter 1

I had been told it was a growth, as naturally as I was offered another cup of tea. I felt no alarm, no deep gloom, no sickening pang of regret, no definite dread of death – at least, not at first. I had been in hospital many times previously. Once I was attacked with a knife and beaten up so badly that it took three operations before I could return to work. Then I had an allergic reaction to penicillin and nearly died – oh yes, I was well versed in all the bureaucracy and sterility of hospital life. The endless tedium of dressings, injections, wheeling of trolleys to and fro, nurses darting hither and thither carrying their ominous kidney-shaped dishes. Interminable conversations that one never has elsewhere. Daily talk of bowels and of passing water, of enemas and catheters. I hated it all, but the worst of it was being trapped. I was in no doubt that genuine kindness prevailed in such institutions, but to me it was a friendly tyranny that I was forced to endure because I had forfeited my right to control my life.

True, I had entered the ward with little remonstration, having first made a whimsical show of defiance in naming a bishop friend as my next-of-kin. Under relationship on the form I put 'Father'. I wondered if that would foul up the computer and continued most unadvisedly with the nurse when she began her statutory list of questions: 'Are you allergic to anything?'

'Yes, hospitals.' She ignored this.

'What are you in for?'

'My sense of humour.'

She ignored this valiantly. 'They've got to take it out. It's cancerous.' That word signified death.

Death was out of the question for I still had five hundred thousand pounds to raise. I was planning a new project to help bright but disadvantaged lads of sixteen, and it would be the crowning glory of Project Spark, the scheme for delinquent children I had set up in my home. As I drifted in and out of consciousness, the faces of some of the Spark kids blinked over me at queer angles, like distorting mirrors. Freddy's urchin grin, silhouetted like a half moon, hovered by my pillows. 'Well, you made good didn't you,' I muttered, wondering if that young man was really there beside me. 'So did Piers.' I savoured the smug satisfaction of self-congratulation. 'What was the name of that boy who arrived in Project Spark at the same time as you and had found his baby brother dead, hidden in some blankets in a drawer?' It was eerie, but I could smell the stale flesh and see the social worker grasping that small bundle of rags.

People came and went. I recognised the droning voices around my bed, but could not always put names to the gargoyle faces that loomed intermittently. My mind wandered back to the days before Spark, when I had gone to the States to escape the attention caused by *Bury Me In My Boots*.

He had sat crosslegged in the Chicago doorway with an old, battered hat cocked on the side of his head. When the policeman routed him out, he rose, slowly. Then, as much as to say, 'Maybe I will, maybe I won't', he yawned again and sauntered off. He walked on and on, oblivious to traffic signals and I walked, wordlessly, at his side. We continued southward until we came to some railroad yards and then from beneath his shaggy black beard, for the first time, my friend spoke.

'This is Hobohemia. It's a good place to loaf. There's coal and wood and plenty of vacant space to build a fire and keep warm. We'll have to be careful of the railroad police, but otherwise . . .

'Well, I've been on the road for a good thirty years, in Europe, in your country, England, but I was born here on South State Street. I went to sea and bummed back here after the war. You weren't even born then were you?' He refused my offer of a cigarette and rolled one of his own.

'I'm a hobo, not a down-and-out or meths drinker, like you wrote about in your book. I'm not a derelict, though like them I'm anti what you call the Establishment. I don't take dope and I don't even drink. I'm just a tramp who likes to keep to myself and travel, and keep travelling. There aren't many of us left. In the old days we came back from the West when they closed the mines and worked the railroads. I stay out of the cities mostly – too dangerous – but I always come back to Chicago. It's the main drag, the railroad centre of the universe or so they say, and you're always passing through.

'I do work sometimes in the winter when it's cold. There's always a casual job in Chicago. But in the summer, never. There's a difference between the down-and-outs and us – perhaps it's the same difference as between society and us. The down-and-out is society – the bottom end of society. Society is what makes him.

'Me, us, the hobo, we're just ourselves. Society makes friends and enemies. We make friends and enemies, but just for the day and then we move on. Home's the road. No, I don't take help from the welfare organisations. I can't take the people who are trying to help – nothing against you of course – but they're wasting their time. You can't preach the drunk out of being a down-and-out. There's too much that went into it before the booze.

'These charities, settlements, missionaries, go at life through a misunderstanding. They don't understand the sociology of Christ. If someone is miserable, don't redeem him. Get off his back.'

He took out his pocket knife and began to scrape the dirt from under his fingernails. 'I get by. I've good legs, lungs and heart. I've got a good heart.'

I could see he didn't want to talk any more. As the sea calls to the sailor, although no part of it is his, so the land calls to the hobo. In an incomprehensible way, he's earth-hungry,

3

although he's always driven off it. It's a hunger that means he never really has any human friends. So it was that we met, then we each went on – alone.

I went to New York to work with the drug addicts, still firmly of the belief that, given the right environment and a little love and understanding, young people often labelled as 'maladjusted' or 'deprived' or simply as 'drop-outs', could be given sufficient self-confidence not only to take their proper place in society, but to be responsive to the needs of others. It was a small coloured boy that confirmed this idealistic quest.

Jake was nine years old when I first met him and like his nine brothers and sisters, he had joined death-row on the streets of Harlem, taking heroin. In the morning the police would raid the gangs to confiscate their drugs, and in the evening would be found discreetly selling back the morning's takings to the desperate youths. To avoid this daily ritual, Jake had taken to hiding on the flat roofs of the derelict tenement buildings where in the shadows of the chimneys he would spend the day snorting his illicit haul. One warm afternoon we were lounging up there when a man of the cloth, identified by a dog collar, approached us. The large, lumbering, big-boned Man of God halted and listened to the rasping breath of my small friend.

'Son, do you go to church?' he finally drawled.

Jake wiped his runny nose on his sleeve and, without looking up, replied 'Nah, sir.' The big man pondered.

'Do you read the Bible?'

The child reflected on this as his bony hand placed the heroin in the back pocket of his too-big shorts for his wasted body. 'Nah, sir,' he replied.

With no tenderness and no new subtlety the man continued, 'Do you have any kind of religion at all, son?'

Unwrapping his spindly legs from beneath him, Jake stood up and, sticking out his weedy chest, looked up at the lamenting preacher and said with mild consideration, 'Yeah, sir, I'm a black Christian.' His inheritance secured, the child, untroubled, meekly lowered his curly black head and stared at his naked feet. The Godlike mortal before us sighed deeply as if mourning for the world's woes and cried

4

balefully, 'Learn to know the Lord, son, you are just black.' I was on my feet with my arm raised before he could utter 'Alleluia'. His holy nose was in my sight and my clenched fist was about to come to eternal rest upon it when my young friend placed a firm restraining hand on my elbow and gently said, 'Sal, don't hit him – even the adequate need understanding.' Jake was dead five years later and I had married, inherited six stepchildren, given birth to two boys, and founded Project Spark in Jake's memory.

Since my work among the drop-outs of the 1960s, I was convinced that prevention was better than cure. Then I had watched teenagers destroy their lives with alcohol and drugs and experienced the futility of being unable to offer much practical help, apart from unconditional love. I knew it was not enough and my travels across America confirmed it. So it was that in 1973, and separated from my husband, I came to London with my younger children, where we rented a house not far from Hampstead Heath. It has been our home for the last sixteen years and it has, just as important, been a second home for many youngsters like Freddy and Piers, Ricky and Martin – a sanctuary for the distressed, an oasis for the oppressed – and a life's work for me. Under this roof rose Jake's temple, his spring of hope, his well of deep understanding – all the nourishment for the children of Project Spark.

The mechanics of setting up the Spark Charity were straightforward. I formed a trust with six trustees to handle all the money I raised and then registered the newly-formed project with the Charity Commissioners and appropriated the pompous title of director. When all the legal documents were signed and sealed I ventured down to the local comprehensive school which my stepdaughter was now attending. The headmaster was small in stature, a ginger-haired man who bubbled benevolently from behind his horn-rimmed glasses. I came directly to the point. 'I have a proposition for you.' His eyes twinkled.

'Really! I haven't been propositioned by a young lady for some time.' I blushed.

'Sorry, I didn't mean it quite like that. What I meant was that I know you are aware of my past work with delinquents

5

and I wondered if you'd be agreeable if I put it to good use in your school?'

'Explain yourself.'

'Well . . . I've got this large house round the corner and you have some difficult kids, who can't or won't fit into the system. I wondered if we couldn't marry the two.' He took off his glasses and cleaned them with his handkerchief.

'Go on.'

'Well . . . I believe if we can catch your problem children young enough and put them in a loving, small, caring environment for a couple of terms or even a year, we could bring about a fundamental change in them. I'm prepared to try it, if you are.' He laughed genially at me.

'My dear lady, I am a tiny cog in a very large wheel called the Inner London Education Authority. I cannot sanction anything outside their system. Anyway, what would you do with them from nine till four every day?'

'What you do – teach them.'

'Are you a qualified teacher?'

'No, but we could invest in one if we have to comply with ILEA rules.'

'From where? All my monies are allocated for the year.' I could feel my blood rising in hot temper.

'Look, I was told you were a go-ahead, far-sighted headmaster and if you can't see the benefits of this idea to your school, I'll try someone else.' He raised a hand to placate me and motioned me to silence as only an authoritarian can.

'My dear, I think there are possibilities here, but I don't think you've thought it through. I'll tell you what, go and put it on paper and then let's look at the idea again.' Feeling like one of his first-years, I went home determined to write a detailed report to put on his desk as a first-class piece of homework for the next morning. In fact I handed it to his secretary at eight fifteen and sat by the phone the remainder of the day. He rang me that evening and informed me that he would like me to meet him, his deputy head and the head of discipline and pastoral care the following afternoon after school. At last he was taking me seriously.

The three professionals and myself sat for hours discussing

my report, occasionally lubricating ourselves with coffee and, as the late afternoon turned into evening, whisky. At the end of the day there were still two major problems – my lack of qualifications and the school's lack of finance. We succumbed to exhaustion with the two problems unsolved.

It was a few days later that I bombed into the head's office. His secretary, appalled at my lack of respect, gave me a withering glare as I pounced unannounced on the busy man.

'I've got it. I know how we can get round it,' I shouted gleefully, falling into his best armchair. He blinked at me over the top of his spectacles. 'We don't tell anyone and I don't get paid,' I announced triumphantly.

'My dear,' he said soothingly, 'what exactly do you mean, we don't tell anyone?'

'Exactly what I say. If I take this on unpaid, as a volunteer, just as you have parents coming in to help in special education, no one need know. I mean, what's the difference except instead of me coming into school, the kids come to me.'

'But you admitted the other day you needed the income to pay the bills.'

'Well, listen to this. You send me four kids for a term for two days a week. They come on condition they attend school the other three days. I can support my family on some part-time job. Now if I can return these four kids to school up to standard in their work and able to behave and not truant, would you be prepared to go to the big white chiefs of ILEA and tell them that you want them to support and finance Project Spark as an off-site unit for your school? If at the end of that trial period I fail to help these disturbed children, I promise I will never bother you again. This way you have nothing to lose and I've got everything to prove.'

He hesitated.

'Sally, I am about to interview a parent whose child I'm intending to suspend. Would you please . . .'

'Terrific! Can he be my first pupil?' I interrupted. His face was turning puce and his voice had risen a decibel.

'Sally, that's enough. I will discuss it with my two senior

staff when I have time, which I do not have now. Would you please leave my office?'

I rose from his chair cheerfully, 'Okay, okay, calm down. I'm leaving, but . . .' I grinned winningly and gave him the V sign, calling back over my shoulder as I passed the fretting parents, 'Go for it man, go for it.'

Chapter 2

I was sent four bovver-booted horrors. I had hoped for second-years, aged twelve, who would be small and more malleable, but in came these long-haired, six-foot louts with chains bedecking their necks and wrists. They stood in my drawing-room, taking up the entire space as I sat there staring at the holes in their jeans, feeling small and insignificant.

'Wot we been sent 'ere for?' Blondie demanded gruffly. I chose my words carefully.

'You haven't been sent – you're here voluntarily, you can leave any time you like . . .' Blondie turned to his mates.

'Yer 'eard the lady, let's go' and they began to file out. The dismay on my face halted the last lad. His heavy-lidded eyes looked at me half sorry, half disgusted. He slightly opened his thick lips and deliberately pursed them, blowing me a kiss as he squashed a spider into the carpet with his boot. I'm like that insect, I thought, a nothing to be so easily crushed. My battered pride was seized with indignation.

'Hold it you guys – give me a chance will you? Please . . . let me make some coffee and we'll . . .' I was rudely interrupted by Blondie who stood at the open front door.

'Coffee? – lady we drink beer – got it – it's four letters B, E, E, R – see lady, I can spell, I don't need no f——— teacher.'

'Okay, okay, you guys, beer it is. Come back, I have some lager in the kitchen,' I heard myself saying, as I thought what on earth am I doing offering them beer at nine-thirty in the morning? Not to mention it's illegal – they're all under sixteen. I pointed this out. They laughed.

'We've been drinking beer since the age of seven,' Thick Lips said.

'How did you get it?'

'Stole it,' said the brute on my left.

'Yes, of course, how silly of me,' I replied in a deflated tone.

'Got an ash-tray then?' Blondie asked, and I found four ash-trays. Through the haze of smoke, Brute asked, 'So wot yer goin' to do wiv us?'

'Well that's as much up to you as it is to me,' I declared democratically. 'You see the point is, or at least so I gather, that you truant from school and that's breaking the law . . .' Hoots and cheers followed, and when the noise had subsided I continued, 'Well you might think it's clever, but in fact it's rather stupid . . . you . . .'

'Yer calling us stupid?' Blondie cut in aggressively.

'No, anyone who can beat the system all these years can't be stupid, but your behaviour is, for you're cutting off your nose to spite your face.' They stared at me in silence.

'Wot yer mean?'

'Well, by not attending school who gets hurt? The teachers don't.'

'We don't.'

'Well, that's where I disagree with you. If you can't read or write properly or fill in forms to collect social security, who's the loser?' Their glasses were empty and I knew they were waiting for me to fill them. 'You see, by truanting you're actually helping the school because when you're present your behaviour is so disruptive, the teachers find it impossible to teach so they are delighted when you don't turn up.'

'So why do yer want us?' I was about to answer when the kitchen door was nudged open. 'Bloody hell! Wot's that?'

'Wot do yer fink it is, a bloody camel?' Blondie was on his feet.

'Nah, it's a dog,' said Thick Lips. Suddenly they had all left the table, forgotten about their empty glasses and were crowding round Dog.

' 'Ee's a beauty,' said Blondie.

'Look at 'is size – bet 'e's a good watch-dog, miss.' I was amazed. All their aggression and macho behaviour had disappeared in an instant. Suddenly they were human teenagers.

'Wot's 'is name?' a voice from the fourth lad, who so far hadn't spoken.

'Good heavens! You can speak,' I teased. They all turned away from Dog and stared at me. I grinned back good-humouredly and suddenly all their faces beamed back. I knew I had won, or at least Dog had, in more ways than one, for his walks increased four-fold over the term.

I was quite apprehensive whether they would show up for their second session of the week, but on the dot of nine o'clock, they clinked through with their metallic chains and bracelets into the kitchen. I had mugs of steaming coffee waiting for them.

'Not drinking that,' Blondie stated.

'Suit yourself,' I replied dismissively.

'Where's Dog?' Wordless asked.

'He's in the garden, you can let him in if you want.' Everybody rose to let the animal in, and an ecstatic reunion followed.

'Now, look you guys, we've got to make a plan of action for the term. What, for instance, are your hobbies?'

'Sex and boozing.' Blondie was the spokesman, of course. I deliberated.

'Well, I can't do anything about the sex' – guffaws of laughter – 'but I do have an idea about the booze. There are two conditions. One, that you stop stealing it and second, you have to attend here regularly and be prepared to do the work I set for you.'

'Wot, yer going to give it to us?' They looked amazed.

'No, it's not quite as straightforward as that. We're going to make it and in the process you're going to learn your tables and weights and measurements.' Blondie swore in disbelief.

'And that's another condition – no unnecessary swearing in this house. It's most unpleasant to listen to and it's not good for Dog to hear. I don't want him picking up your bad habits.'

11

So twice a week we all settled into an amiable routine of coffee and Dog-greeting followed by English, often in the form of a word game. Break at eleven for a game of snooker in the hall or playing with Dog in the garden, followed by a maths lesson in the form of making beer. The head rang me occasionally or would pop round to see if I was still alive and on one occasion we invited him to lunch. Little did he know he drank the beer that the boys had made on these premises over the last few months. As the term came to an end, we held a farewell party at which I dropped the bombshell.

'Well guys, this is the end of the road. You've got to go back to school next term, and I mean, not part-time.'

'Can't we go on coming 'ere?'

'No – the agreement was a term, but I'd love to see you after school. In fact, I've got an idea. What about if you go back to school and for every week you attend, not missing a day, you can come here on Friday and tell me all about the week and collect a bottle of beer.'

'Wot if we miss a day?'

'No beer.'

'Wot if we're thrown out of our lessons?'

'I'll be very angry – you're as good as the next guy and you can behave better. Anyway if you do – no beer.'

'That's called blackmail, miss.'

'Indeed not – it's called encouragement,' I announced. 'And I shall ring the school every week and talk to your housemasters, so don't think you can get away with anything. You might be able to beat the system, but you're not going to beat me.'

'Nah, miss, we wouldn't try it on wiv yer.'

My four bovver-booted louts returned to school. The headmaster agreed I was a genius and rushed round to ILEA to declare his find and seek financial help for his school's off-site unit called Project Spark One. By the end of the school year we had turned the large dining-room into a schoolroom, had the fire brigade round to screen us for fire precautions, advertised for a teacher, turned the garden into a play area for badminton or volley ball and the garage into a workshop for woodwork and tinkering with bicycles. Despite my lack of qualifications I was offered the post of educational welfare officer to the Spark unit and the grand sum of three and a half thousand pounds a year. In 1975 we were sent our first twelve problem children aged eleven to thirteen. Over the next four years I was to realise that the needs of the older children also were insufficiently met, so in 1979 Spark Two was established for fourth- and fifth-year problem pupils in my converted bedroom upstairs, and another qualified teacher was employed.

The very nature of the problems which our Spark One pupils experienced in school meant they often lacked confidence in basic educational skills. Therefore our primary aim was to concentrate on the 'three Rs' in order to settle them into a pattern of discipline and work. Once this was established, we broadened their horizons. Teaching was highly disciplined, but with much tender loving care and because of our framework of individual caring, we developed a sense of loyalty, respect and old-fashioned courtesy within our children. We found that a natural progression from this was an increased self-respect and an ability to adjust to problems, a new-found self-confidence to cope within society and therefore the possibility of returning to full-time school, often within the year.

Our aim for the older children in Spark Two was not to return them to full-time school, but to help them complete their final two years in education with as few problems and as many exams as possible. The maximum number of children we would take was ten. This was due to limited space and the number of children we felt we could help without them being 'lost' in the group. In some cases a child simply moved from Spark One to Spark Two, but in most cases a new child's name and history was put forward at our weekly referral meetings.

If we felt the child was suitably motivated and that the kind of environment we offered was suitable for him and his problems, he was accepted. Then consultation with the parents, the social services, the probation officers and others would take place. Finally, we would venture into the child's school to confer with his head of house, year tutor and individual teachers to find out in which subjects that child was particularly disruptive or under-achieving. Wherever possible we tried to keep the children in their exam lessons, but inevitably the problems were often serious and the child would have to be withdrawn. From this we established an individual timetable for each child, with some time in school and some time in Spark.

We approached these children as young adults and dealt with many of their problems simply by reasoning and talking. For the nonconformist, standard punishments were used. A child made up lost time after school hours if found truanting, and each child could earn an outing of his choice once a week. If they misbehaved or were ill-mannered, then that privilege was withdrawn. The group 'knitted' together and became a very close unit. This was helped by the fact that each day one child cooked lunch for the rest. They had to shop and prepare a two-course meal. Therefore, each day we sat down together and ate very well! During this time many things were discussed, sorted out and arranged, but in most cases it formed relationships and they learnt basic social skills – using a knife and fork! Teachers and welfare workers were often invited to lunch and this gave them a chance to see and be seen by the children in a relaxed context where problems could be more easily discussed. Apart from the academic and social skills which were all-embracing in Spark, in the last school year we let every child out on work experience for one or two days a week, and every summer the juiciest morsel of our carrot-and-stick system was the annual holiday. Twelve Spark kids could go away for a week's adventure holiday, but had to earn their place by good work and behaviour. Once we stayed in a converted cowshed at the foot of Snowdon, another time we rode horse-drawn wagons across Dartmoor and there were abseiling and sailing in Devon.

As the summer holidays approached and exams were finished it was difficult to motivate the Spark children to work. One particular boy was giving us grave concern and I knew that I had to make a decision about his future within a few days. He had been sent to us from his school last term and we found his behaviour increasingly more disturbed and disturbing. His school reports were a sure recommendation to Spark:

14

English   I found Edward's behaviour uncontrollable and irrational right from the first term. He never seems to comprehend why he has been singled out for punishment and even when he is spoken to individually he does not seem to understand how disruptive and antisocial his behaviour is. He is loud-mouthed, swears at the top of his voice without provocation and bullies and manipulates other children in his class.

French   Edward's behaviour in class leaves a lot to be desired. He talks to his friends, reads comics, fiddles with pen or pencil, in fact does everything but work. He cannot accept criticism, and either does not understand or is unwilling to understand what he has done wrong. He is rude to me and his classmates and always tries to disrupt when the others are working. He is having a very undesirable effect on the group and it is very noticeable what a great improvement there is in the classroom when Edward is not present.

Geography   I think Edward is the *rudest* boy it has ever been my misfortune to meet in a first-year group. The amazing thing is that he has been this way from the very first lesson onwards. He often arrives late for lessons, usually ignores me and starts to talk to his cronies in the room. He rarely arrives with his exercise-book, and even less frequently does he have pen, pencil or ruler. Far from being apologetic about this, he is actually rude about it. During a lesson Edward will often make stupid remarks – it is as if he cannot bear to sit in a room which is quiet – he has to disturb. I did notice a remarkable difference in class atmosphere last term when Edward was absent.

Drama   As far as I'm concerned Edward has made no effort to come to terms with this subject, with me or the rest of the class. Most of the time he sits tilting on his chair, aiding or abetting any mischief perpetrated by others, oblivious to any activity or instructions. He keeps apart from the rest of the class and no one seems anxious to befriend him. He is indifferent to even simple things like timetables, he is frequently late if he's there at all, and never does as he is told. I have been unable to get through to him on any count.

Edward was referred to us as the last resort before the

downhill procedure to Special School. He was built like a German Tiger tank. His head was so large that he seemed not to have a neck and his cumbersome, gorilla-like walk automatically made him intimidating. He knew how to use his physique and backed it up with a razor-sharp tongue, recklessly shooting swear words like arrows into the foe. He appeared to know nothing of love or caring, only of society's conspiracies to lay secret snares to wound him. He was no different from a wild animal seeking his own survival in the bush.

I was to discover that Edward had been deprived of all basic childhood emotional and moral support. Every child needs sympathy and kindness and if he grows up in an atmosphere of heartlessness, he, in turn, will be indifferent to goodness, and indifference is the most dangerous mental state of all. Once a child is indifferent it is particularly difficult to restore any self-esteem or inner resources.

Edward's first term with us was most notable for his absence. Daily I would arrive at his home first thing in the morning to collect him only to find he had left the house early to avoid me. When I eventually made contact with his mother, she always announced he was at school. He would roam the streets and I would follow suit in chase. If I found him he would get in the car with sullen submissiveness and I would return him to the Spark classroom where he developed the habit of doing things only at gunpoint. This was not Spark's philosophy. It was always important for our children to sense in the teacher's censure not only justified severity, but also kind concern. As a last resort I withdrew Edward from the classroom. We worked in the garden together; we peeled potatoes for the evening meal together; we went shopping together; we washed and cleaned the minibus together. I talked to him endlessly, trying to build up his confidence and trust, but he closed all his safety valves and gave nothing. He was now in trouble with the police and had reverted to acts of violence. It was the end of the academic year and Edward became one of the very few children we failed to help.

Chapter 3

At the beginning and end of every holiday my children's school vacations coincided with the Spark children's term. Christopher, now fifteen, was away at boarding-school having won an assisted place at Winchester, while Nicholas was a day boy in his first year at public school in London. They had always been involved with the Spark children, for they came on the Spark holidays, and during the vacations the Spark kids had nothing better to do, so turned up on our doorstep to play snooker in the winter or croquet in the summer. My sons treated these kids as I did, as part of an extended family and because they had grown up with the Project in their home, there was an unquestioning acceptance of their presence. I did insist that Nicholas and Christopher had their own private bedrooms, but even they were shared in emergencies, like when Jason ran away from home. I rang his mother to inform her he was safe.

'I don't care a f—— if he's under a lorry – I don't want him back here.'

It was after midnight and the end of the week, so I said soothingly, 'I'll keep him for the weekend. You sound tired. I'll give you a ring on Sunday evening and perhaps we can meet and discuss the problem.'

'It's no f—— problem to me – it's your f—— problem now,' and she put the telephone down. In fact it did not turn out to be a problem at all, for Jason refused to return to his mother and said the only place he wanted to live was with his Nan, and Nan was delighted to have him.

Another unexpected weekend visitor was Tommy, who had problems at home also, and arrived on us the weekend of the Eton/Winchester cricket match. With his Mohican haircut, studded belt and bracelets and DMs, he invaded the Pimms-drinking gentry of the green fields of Winchester and was an enormous success among the boys. He slurped champagne over the picnic, his black leather a devil's contrast to the creased cricket whites of the playing fraternity. I swear this famous annual event had never seen the likes of it before!

When Christopher graced us with his presence I found his clothes equally odd – shirts cut away at the sleeves, a studded belt dipping over such tight jeans that he could hardly walk, and black leather boots laced up to his calves. I always knew when he was home because the fridge was suddenly emptied, the kitchen full of dirty coffee mugs, the washing basket full to the brim and the bathroom unavailable every morning.

'He stands in front of the mirror,' Nicholas explained.

'What, for an hour and a half?'

'He likes himself.' I winced, and muttered that not even Narcissus liked himself that much as I ventured into the schoolroom to see if Shelley was present.

She had been sent to us, aged thirteen, as a school-phobic; at least this was the diagnosis of the educational psychologist. My scepticism was vindicated when she never arrived here either. So I commenced my common routine with such children by going in the car and picking her up – having a chauffeur-driven limousine to collect her did wonders in improving her attendance record! On the surface she appeared a woolly-headed, indolent child, sweet and harmless. She was very pretty with very dark rings under her eyes; why was it that she was never awake in the mornings when I sat outside hooting for her, like an alarm clock? It was only then that it occurred to me that the reason she didn't turn up at school, or with me, was there was nobody in the house to wake her up – her parents were out all night. The next morning, instead of waiting in the car I went to the front door and rang the bell. Clad only in a pair of knickers, the child opened it, and before she could rub the sleep from her eyes I was in with the front door closed behind me.

'Time to get up or we'll be late for Spark.' I cheerfully followed her down the corridor. 'As I'm here, can I have a word with your Mum or Dad and tell them how well you're getting on? Where's the kitchen and I'll make a pot of tea?' She was throwing her clothes on.

'Mum won't be in for another hour and Dad ain't come back yet. The kitchen's opposite the toilet.'

I boiled the kettle as I worked out my strategy to inveigle more information from her, when I opened the large fridge/freezer for milk. I froze in horror. The shelves had been removed and there, coiled round and round, filling the whole refrigerator, was a massive fat python. Trembling, I pushed the door closed, and with a warbling voice cried, 'Come on, we haven't time for tea, we're going to be late,' and dashed for fresh air. Once in the car, having pulled my shaken self together, I calmly said, 'Did you know there's a python in your fridge?' She giggled and replied,

'I know. Dad put it there. He's going to make a snake-skin bikini for his girlfriend. Ever so upmarket don't you think?'

From bitter experience, I learnt that unless I locked up the house and physically removed myself from it I would never have a break from the Spark children. If they didn't want to play snooker, could they take Dog for a walk? It was raining, so could they come in and play table tennis; their television had broken, could they watch with the boys in the drawing-room? Mum was at work and they couldn't get in the house and they hadn't had any lunch, and so it went on. So come the summer holidays, the edifice was locked and barred as if it were Fort Knox and the boys and I followed the sun south. But on my return I always wondered if it was worth it, for there was so much to do: timetables to be sorted out for the Spark children, rugger gear to be bought for Nicholas, name tapes to be sewn on Christopher's new acquisitions, a month's pile of mail on my desk awaiting attention. Haircuts, dentists, chiropodists, had to be organised before the term began; round to the school for pre-term meetings; worksheets written up and xeroxed, equipment for the new term ordered; hatchet bought for garden, in order to see if Tarzan and Jane hadn't moved in.

Always on the day of the new term of the new academic year I was exhausted but buoyant. Hard work it was, but there was also that underlying excitement of the unexpected, for never a day passed that was the same.

It was an inauspicious beginning for Sue, the new teacher in Spark One. The headmaster and I had advertised in the national press the previous term and had short-listed eight possibles. These were asked to attend interviews the following week when I had them in a group for the morning in Spark and over bread and soup and wine chatted to them informally. By the time they lined up for the formal interview with school governors and the head, I had already chosen the appropriate candidate. My prerequisites were different from the school governors'.

I was not interested in erudite or experienced teachers. First and foremost I wanted a teacher who found joy in contact with kids, who truly believed that every child could become a worthwhile human being, someone who could empathise with the joys and sorrows of a child's heart, but had enough common sense not to become emotionally overwhelmed by the impact. Second, I wanted someone who not only had a grasp of the syllabus material, but a range of knowledge infinitely wider than the school curriculum, for I needed a teacher who was in search of new ideas and new material to enrich the lessons that Spark children often found boring in school. Third, I wanted a teacher who was self-disciplined, who therefore not merely told her pupils how to behave, but educated them by example.

On this occasion I had put forward my case for Sue to the school governors and head and they had accepted it. On the third day of her initiation to Spark, Sue came to the drawing-room after school, quite distressed.

'What is the matter?' I asked.

'I think Piers has stolen my car keys – but I can't prove it,' she faltered.

'Why do you think it was Piers?'

20

'When everybody had left the schoolroom, he was hovering by my handbag.'

'That's not exactly evidence – let's go and have a look.' We searched the schoolroom, we searched her bag, we searched the hall and kitchen until she quietly said, 'We're wasting our time – I know exactly where I put them in the handbag and they're not there.' This was a serious misdemeanour and I realised immediately that it could not wait till the morning.

'Leave it with me, Sue. Go home – were your house keys with them by the way?'

'No, fortunately not. What are you going to do?'

'Leave it with me – I'm going to get your keys back.'

'You're not going to call in the police are you?'

'Good heavens, no, now don't worry.' Then another thought occurred to me. 'I hate to mention it, but I suppose your car is still outside?' I moved with clumsy sympathy and patted her shoulder as I led her out to the front door. We stared at the grey Morris Minor in relief.

When Nicholas came in that evening I asked him what he thought of Piers.

'I like him. He's good fun,' he replied casually as he sat at the kitchen table drowning his sausages in tomato ketchup.

'Well, I'm leaving you to finish the clearing because I've got to go over and see him – I'll see you later.'

'Okay, I've got tons of homework.'

I called Piers my OAP as he was eventually one of our longest-serving members in Spark. He arrived as a disciplinary problem from primary school at the age of eleven, progressed into Spark Two and left us at the school-leaving age of sixteen. He was a large, fair boy, who frisked round like a wild unco-ordinated colt. He was unable to sit still for more than five minutes and became impatient with his work, so rushed it. Inevitably it was more often than not wrong, and its presentation deplorable. When this was explained to him he immediately took it as a criticism and would sulk for the rest of the day. He was convinced we were exposing his weaknesses and shortcomings, thus injuring his self-esteem and sense of dignity. He was typical of the child who believed the adult had no respect for him and, because he had no means of demonstrating his moral dignity, he would seek ways of calling attention to himself by disruptive behaviour.

Our philosophy in Spark was that our pupils were not just schoolchildren, but first and foremost they were people in their own right, with a variety of interests, needs and aspirations and that a vital precondition of the relationships between those in authority and those under instruction was to foster, encourage and enhance these desires and ambitions. We welcomed our children as like-minded friends with whom we shared the joys of success and the sorrows of disappointment, thus creating a comradeship between pupil and teacher, for if they see in you one of their equals their guards are lowered and they open up and confide.

Of course, there is an exception to every rule and in our first year with Piers, he proved the salutary example of this! He grew physically into a large, bombastic boy who could not control his moods or actions. He had become totally dishonest and a deplorable sneak. He had no sense of loyalty or responsibility to his friends or the group, and was fast becoming amoral. We called a meeting with his teachers and educational psychologist to discuss what more we could do for him – he was virtually banned from every lesson in school and they were of the firm belief that a move towards special education (i.e. school for the maladjusted) was inevitable.

The Spark staff did not agree and asked for more time. We had discovered he had an enormous talent for drawing, and that, combined with his frequent dramatic physical outbursts, caused us to ask a special favour, that he could join the art and drama classes. This was only agreed on by the meeting if the two relevant teachers agreed. Despite his unwholesome reputation, the teachers consented for Piers to join their classes. School was sceptical, Spark was optimistic! I knew we were playing for time, but whether through pride or an irrational sense of belief in this boy, I wanted to give him another opportunity.

Over the year I had had glimpses of a totally different child. When he thought no-one was watching he had lain down beside Dog, stroking and talking to him in such soulful, gentle tones. Another time, when Nick and Christopher were in bed with some nasty disease, he had slipped into their sick room and showered them with sweets. There was a thread of a tiny path leading to a human heart – I had seen it and it justified my faith in him, and my opposition to the decision to send him to school for the maladjusted.

Slowly but surely over the next year Piers's attitude in Spark changed. His concentration improved, he began to enjoy his maths and his English now was more imaginative and creative. He began to feel secure and his confidence grew. Yet from school we were still receiving gloomy reports of immaturity, under-achieving, poor self-control and discipline, but his art and drama teachers agreed he was not only talented but an assiduous student in their subjects. We were hanging in there and winning; perhaps we became too complacent.

Piers's relationship with his family vacillated according to his moods. His younger brother was at a boarding school for the maladjusted, his sister at primary school. It was a devastating shock to Piers when suddenly he was sent to live with his grandmother when his parents' marriage was in its death-throes. He rapidly deteriorated into his old ways. He became unco-operative and sullen in Spark and behaved so monstrously in drama that his long-suffering teacher declared she could no longer cope with him. I really don't know what would have happened to him if he had not had the support of Spark. Our influence, emotional support and patience counteracted his pain. We confronted him with goodness in our everyday caring and he confronted us with his anger in defence of his anguish. Dare a man dispute the fact that environment has nothing to do with a child's behaviour patterns? For a time, instead of maths or English, we let him take Dog for long walks, sometimes on his own, sometimes I accompanied him and we slowly built him up again. True education, I have learnt, is not just our pupils acquiring knowledge through our teaching techniques, but the ability of the individual to participate in the life of society, or inter-relating with other people. I have come to regard my own education as none other than an increasingly profound awareness of each child in Spark.

I was so distracted by my inner thoughts of how I was to conduct myself that I passed Piers's house twice without realising. Should I be direct and frank and tell him that Sue had accused him of stealing her keys? Should I put it as a rhetorical question and so appear laid back and unconvinced? Should I treat the whole episode as a jocular escapade 'But now, dear Piers, we need the keys back, please?' Or should I appeal to his honesty and loyalty in the group and ask him for help to find the joker who took them? In truth, as I rang the doorbell, all I wanted to do was retreat. I felt unnerved, I wanted to run from this difficult confrontation. The door opened and Piers was standing before me, unsurprised, with a mild expression. I stood resolute, sick in the stomach.

'Can I come in?' I asked. He sniffed and looked uneasily about.

'My dad wouldn't like it.' I kept my eyes on him, trying to will him to respond.

'Fair enough.' Instantly reverting to a lighthearted gaiety I said, 'Piers, we've got a problem. Sue's mislaid her car keys.'

'Wot's that to do with me?'

I felt my voice faltering. 'What happens to anyone in Spark is all our concern,' I replied weakly. He shrugged his shoulders and sniffed again.

'Nuffing to do wiv me,' he replied, slightly too quickly and staring over my head blankly. He folded his arms in such a belligerent way that immediately I realised that I was in a cul-de-sac. I disobeyed my instinct to leave.

'Piers, she's new in Spark and needs all the help she can get,' I pleaded.

'Oh, f—— off!' I knew then that Sue was right, Piers was the culprit.

'Give me the keys, Piers, and let's forget about it.' All congeniality had disappeared.

'Wot keys?'

His insolence discomposed me. 'Look, it's getting late, I want to get home. You've caused enough inconvenience

24

today. Sue had to catch the bus. Give me the keys and we'll talk about it in the morning.' I knew he was not the kind of boy who would change his mind and from his obstinate expression in the half-light of dusk, I knew I had done the unforgivable – I had pushed him into a corner from where, without loss of pride, there was no way out. 'Okay, I'll see you in the morning,' I said uneasily and turned away disgusted with myself. I heard him click the door shut.

I couldn't sleep, I felt anguished. I had failed Sue, I had failed Piers, I'd messed up the whole situation. I turned on my reading light and glared at the ceiling. How could I get through to him now? Indifference he could counteract, kindness he could reject, the police was out of the question. 'The only way to reach that bastard is to give him a bit of his own medicine.' I talked to the grimy yellow lampshade. (Grief! I must go and buy a new one.) Yes, that was the only way he would understand. Dear God, have I really got to lower myself to their level in order to get through to them? As I asked that question I realised what I had to do. Piers's most cherished possession was his bike which he used as daily transport to and from school. Rising from my bed, I threw on my clothes, and thrusting my hands in my pockets I went out into the night.

I parked the car a little down the road from their garage. I moved lightly, with speed, as if I'd known darkness all my life, as if every night of the year I went on a rampage of thieving. There was no moon, I noted, like a professional. As I reached the garage all certainty deserted me. What if I had to break the lock? I felt quite jittery as I fumbled, with my hands on the door. I never did find the lock, for before I could produce the torch from my pocket the door opened. I couldn't believe my luck; it hadn't been closed properly. From the flashlight I could see Piers's bike on the far wall, the wheel chained to its frame. I grabbed it and flung it over my shoulder, peered into the darkness and ran like a rabbit to the car without bothering to close the garage. As I turned the engine, I could feel the sweat breaking out and rivulets running down my back. I was shaking all over. What a lousy burglar I would make, I laughed, in a state of shock. By the time I reached home I had composed myself.

I put Piers's bike in our garage, locked it, and returned to bed.

Not till daybreak did I consider what would happen if Piers called the police. Supposing he didn't come into Spark this morning, what should I do? What appeared to be an inspiration in the middle of the night looked a bloody disaster in the light of day.

Sue was the first to arrive. She was in her mid-twenties, slight of build, with an air of country healthiness in her red cheeks. Her movements and gestures were firm, revealing the self-reliance of a woman with a strong mind of her own.

'Any luck?' she asked. I had decided not to involve her in my nocturnal crime.

'Not as yet, but I'm hopeful. Let's see what the day brings.' I moved towards the kitchen. 'Oh yes, I did see Piers last night. Don't say anything to him.'

'What if he brings the subject up?'

'Play it cool, as if it's all in control.' I laughed nervously to myself – what a shambles; it was all far, far from in control. I wondered if I could go to prison for stealing a bike. I opened the back door so the children could enter when they arrived, rather than having to ring the front-door bell formally. I believed this freedom of entering and leaving fostered a sense of belonging. Sometimes they came in as a group, sometimes individually. It was the latter on this occasion.

Piers arrived last. He was late. His pale face was flushed and his voice jerky. 'I know I'm f—— late. Someone's f—— taken my bike.' He kicked the chair in his fury.

'Well, you know the rules Piers. If you're late you have to make up lost time after school,' I declared in my best schoolmarmish voice.

'It's not my f—— fault is it? Go and find the f—— who nicked my bike, f—— it!' Piers produced a string of foul expletives.

'You don't have to use that language, Piers,' I said sharply.

'F—— off!' He kicked the chair again, which knocked the table, spilling my cup of coffee. Without a word I found a damp cloth and washed the surface and then sat down to read the newspaper. This lack of attention aggravated Piers further.

'You don't bloody care 'cause it ain't your bloody bike.' I continued reading the paper. 'I'll f—— kill the person whose nicked it.' Without looking up I said,

'Piers, you arrived late, you are now wasting time which will be added on to the time after school. Why don't you go into the schoolroom and settle down to your work.' This produced a tirade of abuse, followed by,

'I'm not f—— staying tonight. That's all you f—— care 'bout, whether I'm late, you don't care a f—— about my bike, do you?' I put the paper aside and looked him directly in the eyes.

'You're wrong you know – I do care that you've lost your bike. I do care that you're upset.'

'Nah, yer only care that I'm a precious few f—— minutes late.'

'No, Piers, I care as much about you as Sue.' He looked stunned.

'Wot's she got to f—— do wiv it?'

'Well, when she lost her keys last night I bothered and cared enough to come over to you and get them.'

He blinked at me in astonishment. 'I told yer, I don't know anything about 'er f—— keys.'

'Yes, I know you told me that, but . . .'

'Sal, my bike's been nicked,' he whined. 'That was the most important thing in my life – my grandad bought it for me before he died.' He was struggling to hold back his tears.

'Sue's car is her independence and probably the most important possession in her life.'

'Bet 'er grandad didn't buy it for 'er,' he muttered miserably and, pulling out the chair he had kicked, he sat down. Tears were now freely flowing down his cheeks. Softly I replied,

'I don't know, but I do know her car is desperately important to her and, like you, she was utterly miserable last night when she discovered the keys had been stolen.'

'Yer don't know they've been nicked. She could have left them somewhere.'

27

'No, Piers, someone took them from her handbag and that is stealing.' The tears had ceased. I handed him some kitchen roll.

'Well, I ain't taken them,' he pouted belligerently. The storm was over, even though the truth was not yet unleashed. He glumly stared at my empty coffee mug.

'Do you feel bad?' I asked.

'F—— sick. You know I'd even locked it up. Can't f—— trust anybody.'

'Yes, I know what you mean. That's what Sue felt like last night.' I waited wordlessly. Piers drooped over the table, his shirt rumpled, his face streaked by dried, dirty tears, his volume of abuse dried up.

'Dunno wot my dad's going to say,' he wailed, ' 'cos I was meant to lock the garage door, and I couldn't be bovvered.'

'Piers, your dad isn't going to say anything.' He looked up at me suspiciously.

'Wot yer mean?'

'Because you won't have to tell him.'

'Why?'

'Well, you see, Piers, I know where your bike is.' His drawn breath whistled through the air. I saw neither surprise nor relief in his face, which I had hoped for, but disbelief and hate.

'Where is it then?' he retorted.

'I'm not going to tell you that until you give me the keys of Sue's car.' I had hardly finished my sentence when he wildly jumped to his feet and barked at me, 'Yer f—— bitch!'

'Maybe so, but I should think about it if you want your bike back.'

'Yer cow. You've known all the time that it weren't nicked?'

'Well . . . actually . . . it was nicked.'

'Yer 'aving me on, ain't yer?' he said with an air of anxious relief.

'No, it was well and truly nicked but let's get back to the point – bike for keys.' I held out my hand. Piers glowered. I gave him a maternal smile and in a quiet and charming voice I reasoned, 'When you give me the keys I will give you back your bike.' Normally, I would have insisted that he returned the keys from whom he had stolen them, but by now, though the issue was the same, it had become a personal battle between the two of us.

'Do yer mean, yer nicked it?' he asked quizzically, but calmly.

'Yes.' I felt icy cold inside.

'Do yer know I could 'ave gone to the police?'

'Yes! I could have gone to the police and had you searched, but I haven't.' He nodded in some resentful agreement. We both sat in silence for there was nothing else to say. Suddenly, he put his left hand inside his jacket pocket. With no explanation, but a faint sigh of resignation, he handed me the car keys.

'Follow me.' I led him to the garage and unlocked it. He grinned. 'You can have it after you've made up the time you've wasted this morning.'

'Oh, Sal, yer drive a f—— hard bargain.'

Chapter 4

It was that autumn, with the garden carpeted in a collage of gold and brown leaves, that we acquired two kittens to add to our menagerie. Nicholas was besotted by them, the Spark kids cheered and Dog was deeply aggrieved. The kids made a bed of a cardboard box with a blanket in it, but when we returned from Dog-walking, the cats had totally annihilated it.

After days of discussion, it was agreed to name them Rambo and Rosalinda. To appease the indignation of anti-cat Dog, the kids brought in extra bones collected from the butcher and generally bustled round him. Piers and I had him on Hampstead Heath one afternoon when a heavy-jewelled homespun lady took him for a Bernese Mountain dog. I made a negative gesture and the lady remonstrated, 'But I'm never wrong. I know all the breeds. I've shown at Crufts you know.' I looked suitably impressed but offered no information.

'What's Crufts?' whispered Piers.

'The greatest dog show in the world,' I whispered back.

'Now that I've studied his head of course he's not, he's got collie in him, hasn't he?' she exclaimed.

'No.'

'No collie?'

'No, you're quite wrong,' I assured her.

She changed her vast weight on to the other leg and studied Dog. 'No collie,' she pondered loudly, and then

31

suddenly her large, ugly face cleared. 'I've got it, he's part setter,' she cried triumphantly.

'No, not part – he's all setter,' I announced proudly. She puckered her heavy, elongated brow. 'All setter – with those colours?'

'Indeed,' I replied. 'You must be out of touch – he's a Milton setter.'

She hesitated slightly by drawing in her breath and then swelled as she answered, 'But of course. Come on Oberon,' pulling her white, pugnacious bulldog behind her as, like a ship in reverse, she swept past us.

'Cor, Sal, imagine going to bed with 'er.'

'Imagine living with her.'

'I didn't nah Dog were a Milton setter.'

'He isn't. Dog's father was a Gordon setter and his mother was a beautiful English setter, and Dog . . . well, he was born in the Cotswolds in a small village called Milton.' I was wickedly pleased with myself.

The next morning, at seven-thirty, as Dog opened my door, strolled over to the bed and leapt up to flop over my feet, followed by Rambo and Rosalinda like two clockwork toys, springing across to claw up the duvet, the telephone rang.

It was the school informing me they had an emergency. Emily was thirteen years old and yesterday afternoon had locked her class teacher in the cupboard. The entrapped female now refused to have the child in her class, which seemed reasonable to me. 'I'll keep her for the moment, but until I've seen her mother and all her teachers, I'm really not prepared to commit myself further.'

'No, I quite understand. Will you come round at nine and collect her?' asked the head of discipline and pastoral care.

'No, I can't. At nine I have to be in Fleming House Room where I'm picking up a new boy, Freddy Platts.'

'Oh yes! Have you managed to see his father yet?'

'Yes.'

'So what shall we do about Emily, shall I bring her round and introduce her to Sue and the group?'

'I'd be very grateful if you'd do that. I'll warn Sue.'

Freddy was referred to us a week previously, but I had been unable to make contact with his father about the proposed transfer till a few days before. I had visited the flat five times at different hours of the day and evening, and only on the sixth occasion did I encounter the man. He was lying on the sofa, surrounded by empty bottles, with the television blaring.

'I've come about Freddy,' I shouted, sitting down uninvited, on the only other chair in the room. He was unshaven and sweating profusely. He grunted. 'We think he needs a little more support than the school can give him, so he'll be attending Project Spark, that is if you agree, two days a week.'

This announcement was digested with a swig of the bottle. Finally he said, 'Wot's the nipper dun?'

Once again I explained the position, but his bloodshot eyes were latched to the television. Freddy stood there in the doorway, unsmiling, his empty eyes passing from my face to his father's and there they stuck. No words were exchanged; they didn't need to use language.

Yesterday, I'd received a telephone call from his tutor saying he was refusing to come to Spark, so I had agreed to go to the school. Twelve hundred pupils were littered about the grounds having a fire drill. The new headmaster, whom I could hear but not see, was plaintively screeching like a banshee through a megaphone, 'This is not a game, it is a fire . . .' his voice drowned by the children's jeering. At this point I caught a glimpse of Freddy. He was a small, dishevelled kid with the grey, pinched look of a child who ate too little, slept too little and saw too little sunlight. He was being held by the jacket sleeve by his head of house. I pushed my way through the ill-disciplined hordes and approached the boy. We exchanged suspicious glances. I spoke first.

'Let him go,' I exhorted, ready to put my foot out should he try to run. I grinned and put out my hand to ruffle his tangled mop, but he ducked his head. His eyes were vacant, and there was no trace of a smile on his baby mouth.

'Come on, you don't want me to have to drag you around by the ear, it would look so undignified.' He shuffled his feet forward a foot or so and remained perfectly still. 'Let's go home and get a cuppa.' I turned and slowly walked towards the school gates. The child followed twenty yards behind me.

Emily was there, drinking coffee with the Spark Two teacher, Gloria. Sue obviously had her hands tied up in Spark One and had made arrangements that this well-groomed, highly-sophisticated-looking child was not to be introduced to the rest until break time. She had her reasons, not that I knew them, but I trusted her instincts implicitly, so Gloria had left her class upstairs working and had been left in the kitchen as minder.

'Okay, I'll take over here.' I nodded my appreciation just as Freddy slunk through the open back door. I waved to him to take a pew.

'Okay if I take the minibus this afternoon? We're going bowling,' Gloria announced in her breezy northern accent.

'Fine, as long as Sue doesn't need it.'

'No, I've checked with her, she's taking her lot on the Heath with a picnic and Dog.'

'She's mad; it's a bit nippy for that. Rather her than me.'

'Yes, the bad news is I need you here.' I groaned.

'Who's in trouble?'

'Martin again. He arrived an hour late for school with the excuse that his cat had fallen out of a window from the eighteenth floor and he'd had to take it to the vet, so I rang his mother and they don't have a cat. I told him he's in detention all afternoon for lying and an hour extra after school for being late. You will be here won't you? You haven't got any meetings; well, according to your diary you haven't. I did check first.'

'No, that's fine. He is a silly little liar. Why can't he learn to tell lies that we can't check up on – he's a real thicky, that one.'

Gloria grinned broadly, showing a small gap in her front teeth, her chestnut hair falling below her shoulders in gentle locks.

'Okay. I'll see you later. I'd better go up and see what my little darlings are up to.' She bounced from the room.

'Right you two,' I turned to the two silent kids. 'My name is Sally. Let me tell you about Spark and why you are here.'

Thank goodness it was Saturday tomorrow when I could relinquish my incompatible roles of sinner and do-gooder. Saturday was rest day.

Actually I hated Saturdays. While everyone else lay in bed knowing it was a day off, I had to force myself up to clean the filthy house. At least Nick took Dog out for me at the weekends. By the time I'd cleaned the stove, wiped all the surfaces and washed the kitchen floor, it was lunch time and for the only time in the week all looked pristine. I dreaded the idea that people were actually going to come in and walk across the floor, soil the stove and defile the surfaces, so I sent everyone out to buy fish and chips. It also meant that one could have guests for Sunday lunch while the house was still glowing with superficial cleanliness.

I hated Saturdays, particularly in winter. No one would ring up, presuming I was away for the weekend, which was customary in the summer. Once I'd finished the kitchen, then I was forced to do the drawing-room, so it was preferable not to finish the kitchen. I couldn't clean the drawing-room unless I reduced the disorder on my desk, but working at my desk resembled a weekday, and it was Saturday. I wished someone would ring me up and defuse the boring domesticity. I wondered if the washing was dry, but then I'd have to do the ironing. I ought to feed the animals, but they were asleep on my sheepskin rug and if I disturbed them then I'd have to play with them. If only the telephone would ring – even an obscene call, heavy breathing, anything.

I solved my problem and went scrumping. My neighbour next door was away, so I climbed over his wall and collected all his pears on the ground under his pear tree. Then I remembered seeing some apple trees on the playing fields behind the pavilion, so biked down there. One's not as agile at forty and I had never been very adept at climbing trees, but with much gritting of teeth and heavy breathing I

35

swung myself finally on to a branch. The thought of cooking apple pies, apple strudels, apple crumbles, apple snow, apple sauce, finally convinced me that it was all a big mistake and that I'd really rather go back and see if the washing was dry. I really did hate Saturdays.

Emily settled in immediately. She was confident, bright and extrovert. She burst in one morning with verbal diarrhoea, looking as if she'd come straight from a fashion show. 'Not f—— going to 'er lessons any more, f—— cow.'

'I shouldn't think she'd want you at her lessons if that's how you communicate in class,' I commented as I continued to do my filing. 'By the way is it true that you got suspended last term for hitting a teacher?' She threw her work on the table.

'Yeah. They've changed all my teachers this term 'cause of it – didn't get on wiv them last lot,' she declared somewhat truculently.

'You don't appear to be doing particularly well with this new set of teachers.'

'It's that f—— teacher in textiles – she's too f—— old to teach.'

'Oh, her, you're talking about! Actually she's just had a baby.'

'See wot I mean, too f—— old!' I decided silence was the better part of valour.

Freddy was a different kettle of fish. He was a child filled with fear and resentment. His mother was dead and he had spent much of his young childhood in and out of foster homes, depending on whether his father was in or out of prison. Nor had there been any constancy in his education, for as he moved from one home to another, he moved primary schools. Now thirteen, with a feather-like body, he reminded me of a bird floating and moving with the air currents and sleeping on the wing, hiding from the hawks and eagles and birds of prey. He chose to isolate himself from the group, which caused them to be suspicious. For this very reason, I withdrew him from the classroom sometimes, hoping that I could build a one-to-one relationship, which might appear less threatening, though the teachers were not too thrilled with me on these occasions for he was well behind in his work. His reading ability was of an eight-year-old. On this morning, we had taken Dog for his run in a small park off Hendon Way. We were jogging round the perimeter, Freddy breathing easily and myself gasping and spluttering for air. On the opposite side of the park I saw a teenage West Indian on a racing bike and as he sped past a clump of hedges, he threw something into them. He looked furtively round before pedalling out on to the road.

I noted the spot. 'This way Freddy, let's take a short cut across.' When we reached it I parted the greenery and extracted a two-foot hacksaw. We stared at it. It looked menacing.

'Put it back,' Freddy said sternly.

'Did you see that kid on the bike hide it there?'

'Nah, but it ain't anything to do wiv us – put it back.'

'I think we ought to take it to the police station and explain how it got here.'

'Nah, nah,' he cried in frenzy, his eyes like two marbles, wide with fear.

'Calm down Freddy, what's the matter?' Was it a reaction to the suggestion that we should go to the police or did he know more?

'Put it back, Sal. If we're caught carrying it we'll be nicked for possession of stolen goods.'

'Come off it,' I laughed at him, but he was not smiling.

'It's only our word against theirs.'

'You must have had a bad experience with the police,' I provoked consciously, placing the hacksaw back in the hedge, 'they're not all bad guys you know.'

'They're pigs,' he exploded, and sprinted away. I wondered how I was ever going to get to the bottom of Freddy.

It was not too long after this episode, that Emily was in further trouble. I was rung up by her housemaster and asked to deal with her accordingly. Apparently she had bunked off her English lesson and left the school premises with a couple of friends, to go down to the local grocer's to play on his fruit machines. According to the version she gave me, the

Pakistani grocer put his hand in her friend's pocket. The girls remonstrated, so the man shut down the fruit machines they were playing on. This provoked the girls into further action, and one of them clawed him with her nails while my little darling found a stick to beat him over the head. The Pakistani pushed them out before picking up some tins of food and throwing them at the girls as they retreated. Spark Girl then attacked him with her stick and the Pakistani was last seen running down the road, dropping his ammunition of tinned dog meat, followed in hot pursuit by Spark Girl waving stick.

It all sounded like something out of a Laurel and Hardy silent film, but it actually happened. So I had her up before me after lunch, before they all went canoeing. Friday afternoons are treat times. If the children have worked well and behaved themselves in Spark and in school I reward them with an outing of their choice at the end of the week. Canoeing had been chosen on this occasion.

'Well, you're not going,' I told her. 'You're staying with me and working. I don't like outsiders ringing me up and telling me how badly my kids behave. You don't deserve a good time after threatening people in the street.'

'It weren't people – it were a f—— Paki.'

'I don't care if he was the colours of the rainbow, the point is you don't go around attacking the public – it makes you a menace to society,' I reprimanded.

'F—— mind-bender,' she mumbled, so that I wasn't sure I'd heard correctly.

'What did you say?'

'He's a f—— mind-bender, ain't he?' I had never heard this expression before and couldn't help thinking how unusual it was.

'Whether he is or isn't is totally irrelevant to the issue. I'm not concerned about his problems but yours, and at that time of day you should have been in your English lesson in school. Shouldn't you?'

'Yeah, Sal, but Harry's dad died so we'd gone down to the florists to order them flowers for the funeral.'

'Who the hell's Harry?' A new variant to investigate.

'The son of the corpse.' She held my eyes with a deadpan

expression, but I had had enough of her manipulation and wasting of my time.

'You'll be a corpse in a minute if you don't get your backside into the schoolroom. No outing for you this week.' She would certainly pass her advanced level in contrariness, I mused.

Chapter 5

The year passed quickly and in July we were able to send ten of our Spark One children back to full-time school, up to standard and with few behavioural problems. Freddy, Emily and Piers moved up into Spark Two to become the nucleus of a new group because most of the previous members had taken their final examinations and left. Their exam results were excellent and some even had found employment before knowing their results. Our attendance in the year had averaged ninety-five per cent and we were gloating! But all was not well farther afield.

The education system was in disarray, and teachers were striking for more pay. For reasons of communication and information the Spark teachers and I always attended the weekly staff meeting in school. These had deteriorated from practical sessions to political haranguings, often being adjourned as tempers boiled over. There was a deep sense of dissatisfaction among the teaching profession across the country, and London was no exception. At one of these meetings we were informed that from the next week no lunches would be provided as the teachers now refused to supervise the lunch hour.

This did not affect Spark Two, who cooked their own meals, but the younger ones always went back to school for lunch. Piers suggested that we ran a cafeteria from Spark for the rest of the school, putting all profits back into Spark. The thought of twelve hundred pairs of feet coming through my home, whatever the profits, was as horrendous as the idea of World War Three.

Meanwhile, Gloria faced me with a new problem. A new boy in Spark Two called Riki. A week before, we had discovered he was being met at the school gates after school by a nineteen-year-old Spanish lad, who took him out for meals and occasionally back to his flat. Riki's parents were separated and, not having his father's phone number, I rang the mother. I tried, in vain, to contact her for two days, so when I saw Riki next I made a point of saying that I had tried to reach her.

'It'll have been an expensive call, she's in New York,' he said.

'So who's looking after you?'

'Dave.' I presumed this was the mother's boyfriend.

'When's your mum coming back?'

'Not for another week.' I had left it at that, reckoning on contacting her after she returned. But next day Riki was absent, so I rang his home and Dave answered.

'Yes,' he assured me, he had left at the right time this morning to go to school.

'But he hasn't been at school all day,' I remonstrated.

'Oh dear, and this is just after his father called to tell me that all his lighter fuel has disappeared.'

'I thought you said you were in charge of him? He's not staying at his father's?'

'No, he's staying here, but he's got keys to his dad's flat and he can go over there any time he likes.'

'No one seems to be responsible for this kid. He's running amok. I mean, where is he at the moment? It's four-thirty in the afternoon. Where should he be?'

'I dunno. I just make sure he comes home at night.'

'Great! You're sure he was there last night, since he's been missing today? Anyway, can you get hold of his father and get him to ring me as soon as possible?'

Within the hour his father rang me and I repeated my fears. He was under the impression that Riki came home directly from school and Dave would babysit for the evening, so I pointed out that I had rung continuously for two evenings where no one had answered because no one was in.

'I'm going to get to the f—— bottom of all this. I want to know what's going on. Anne's coming back tomorrow and before she goes to Italy on Saturday she and I are going to have to sit down and sort this out,' the father said. When he finally put the receiver down he had aired all his worries about Riki and his dissatisfaction at his ex-wife's arrangements. Early evening he rang again to say that Riki had returned to his mother's place and that he was on his way over there. He would keep me informed of the situation.

Five phone calls later, two from his father, one from the babysitter and one from a stepbrother I didn't know he had, and finally a distraught and confused one from Riki, left me in no doubt I had disturbed a hornet's nest. Not to mention that now I had learnt that the mother was only home for the next two days before disappearing to Italy for a week. I arranged to meet with the parents in the next twenty-four hours. As far as I was concerned we had to sort out a place of safety for him to stay while his mother was away, or I should be forced to use my professional status as an educational welfare officer and call in the social services.

Riki's father came to see me alone. He had on black leather trousers with pink socks and a shirt with clumps of red roses dotted over it. His hair was like the curly branches of a willow tree, falling to his shoulders, and his John Lennon glasses balanced precariously on his pink nose. I caught the eye of Gloria and suppressed a smile. He sat down in the armchair and produced a notebook into which he proceeded to write every detail of our conversation. He was quizzing me about his son when to my horror I saw Rambo climb up the back of his chair and start playing with his long, blond ringlets. I froze as I heard him say, 'You know, he's got us by the short and curlies.'

I stared at this incredible hair and watched Rambo playfully paw at it. He continued, 'He's got us chasing round in circles, none of us knows where he is or what he's doing.' Rambo was now dancing on two legs with a ringlet in each paw. I began to laugh hysterically as the father, not aware of Rambo, carried on.

'You know this is a very serious situation.' I tried very hard to stifle my giggles and pull myself together, but Gloria was now in convulsions as this wretched cat, fascinated by all this hair, played flick the curlies. I rose, explaining Rambo was behind him, and heard myself say, 'I suppose he thinks it's a lavatory brush.' Gloria guffawed and rolled tortuously on the sofa.

'Oh dear! I didn't quite mean it like that.' How could I make such a personal remark to a parent. I breathed deeply and restrained an impulse to smack my own face. I sat down in a state of controlled shock.

'I knew there was something very wrong,' Riki's father persisted as if we were all quite normal, 'when I got back to my flat and found the boy had cut my teddy bear to pieces.' Gloria was doubled up with tears pouring out of her eyes when my gaze of disbelief met hers. I exploded, my hysteria inspired by Gloria's spasms opposite. I tried desperately to compose myself as I heard him mutter more to himself than us 'and it was my favourite teddy bear'. I laughed till I ached.

Meanwhile my teacher was stoically regaining her poise, and with a deadpan expression observed, 'You know, really it's quite amazing how normal he is considering . . .' I gurgled as I was too breathless to laugh any more. I couldn't believe what I was hearing. How could a parent sit with two strange females and admit that he was upset because his son had knifed his favourite teddy bear. I recovered my equilibrium and tried to look grave.

His father finally said, 'I think the best thing is that if his grandparents agree to have him while his mother's in Italy, he stay there and not come to school. Let him cool down. I'm scared that he might push off – he doesn't care about anybody at the moment.'

'That's why I think it's better he doesn't come to school – it's only for five days and at least we'll all know where he is,' I encouraged.

'You mean mini-house arrest?' his father retorted. 'He won't like that. You know he's really messed us all around hasn't he?'

'No,' I emphasised icily. 'I don't think that's quite the right expression to use in the light of this experience. Personally, I think you as his parents, should question your roles. Have

44

you been fully responsible? Do you think you've passed the buck? If he is messing us around, is it possibly because someone has messed him around. Right?'

'Yeah,' he replied dispassionately, 'yeah, we've all been misled.' At which point the phone rang. I left the drawing-room and took it in the hall.

'Sally is that you?' I recognised the voice, but couldn't place it. 'It's Richard. Have you seen *The Times* today?' Richard was one of my trustees.

'No, I haven't had time. Why?'

'I'm sorry I have to be the bearer of sad news but Leslie died two days ago.' I felt quite numb. The chairman of Project Spark had not only been an ardent supporter of our work, but a good friend to me. I met him while sitting on a youth committee. I was living in York at the time and had just acquired a Labrador puppy. I had driven down to London for my first committee meeting with Pup, a toothbrush and a tin of Lassie, should I decide to stay overnight. I knew no one on the committee except for Lord Longford. As we proceeded through the agenda I observed my fellow committee members in their city suits, and noticed I was the only female present.

Suddenly I realised I hadn't fed the puppy which I'd left asleep in the car, nor did I have a tin opener; it was quite late in the evening and the shops would soon be closed. The annual accounts, which I did not understand, were being discussed when I wrote on a scrap of paper, 'Have you got a tin opener?' and passed it surreptitiously to the tall, distinguished gentleman on my left.

He placed a monocle in his right eye and peered at this over all the typewritten papers in front of him. Underneath my message he wrote, 'No, what for?' and slipped it back to me.

'For my tin of Lassie,' I wrote and once again passed it to my left. Wordlessly, he turned and studied me, allowed the monocle to drop and slowly wrote his reply. It said, 'If you're that hungry, I'll take you out to dinner after the meeting.' It was the beginning of a very special and humorous relationship with Leslie Prince, CBE, which lasted the rest of his life, together in Spark.

The memorial service was held in the Liberal Jewish Synagogue. From a distance I saw Lord Longford and one of my ex-trustees, David Astor, the ex-editor of the *Observer*, who had much admired Leslie's patient control over this wild and bull-headed young woman, who passionately believed in the ideas of Project Spark. Having paid my respects to his widow I returned home deeply saddened.

Within minutes of my walking in I had a phone call from Winchester College to inform me that Christopher had been carried off the games field and was now in the sanatorium with a suspected torn ligament and probably wouldn't be able to play football for the remainder of the term. I sat down at my desk and sent him a get-well card and then rang my accountant to organise a trustee meeting in the near future in order to elect a new chairman.

In the background I could hear Emily. We had picked up a rumour from the police that she was involved with drugs and Gloria was confronting her with it – 'Bet it was that f—— black kid who told yer,' I heard. I thought how ironic that there is such racialism in comprehensive schools, whereas in public schools it is the reverse. White children hold the coloured children in awe, as usually they come from very wealthy parents and, more often than not, superior backgrounds. Gloria came in, disturbing my thoughts.

'How was the memorial service?'

'Simple – as Leslie would have liked it.'

'You look tired.'

'I'm always tired,' I grinned back. 'So what did Emily have to say – apart from her racialist attack?'

'Oh! I ignore those. Personally, I don't believe the rumour and she hotly denied it, though, of course she would.'

'I agree with you. But we'd better keep a closer scrutiny of her. If you hear or see anything out of the ordinary let me know.'

It was Sue who noticed something out of the ordinary in Spark One. Tony had been with us a term. He was a gaunt, solitary boy who had a habit of spitting every time he finished a sentence, but fortunately if he spoke more than one sentence in the week we regarded ourselves as favoured. He had an irritating habit of swaying in his chair, rocking

46

backwards and forwards with his eyes rolling back into his head until only the whites showed contrasting brightly with his black skin. I was at my desk when Sue flung herself into my armchair. Dog moved across to sit at her feet.

'You've come to tell me that I should be thinking about school reports,' I anticipated.

'No, but you should be, now you come to mention it.' We laughed. 'I'm worried about Tony. Have you seen a change in him?' I thought for a minute.

'No, I don't think so, not that I've seen a lot of him recently, not since he spat on the carpet and I went for him.' Sue deliberated.

'I can't put my finger on it, but something's wrong.' I put down my pen and swivelled my chair round to give her my full attention.

'How do you mean? Has his behaviour changed?'

'No. He's not really a behaviour problem because he just sits there. He's not in the least disruptive, just silently unco-operative,' she considered and then added, 'Actually that's not true either – he's not unco-operative, he'll do what I tell him. He's secretive.'

'The school said he was an introvert.'

'I accept that, but this week something has changed.'

'Just this week?' I asked.

'Just the last two days,' she affirmed.

'If it's not his behaviour . . .'

'Well, not what you mean by his behaviour. He did fall asleep over his books this morning.'

'So your teaching technique is so poor that you're driving the children to sleep in your lessons,' I baited. She threw a cushion at me. 'What's his appearance like?' Her eyes lit up.

'That's it.'

'What's it?'

'He used to come in clean. His clothes were dishevelled, but they were clean.'

'You mean, in the last two days they haven't been?'

'That's right, he looks as if he's come straight out of the gutter.'

'Where does he live?'

47

'Not locally.'

'Is his mother on the phone – either at home or work?'

'Can't remember offhand, my book's in the other room.'

'It's okay. I've got mine here.' I opened my desk drawer and withdrew the pale green attendance book. 'No, there's no telephone number. Looks as if I had better pay a home visit.'

'Would you?'

'Yes, I'll pop round after dinner this evening.'

'You don't think we should have a chat with him first,' Sue pointed out.

'We could do, but that can't be till tomorrow unless he's still here.'

'No, he left at three-thirty.'

'Well, it's really up to you. How urgent do you think it is?' She chewed it over and then said,

'I think it's urgent.'

'Okay. That settles it, I'll go tonight.'

I slowly toured the neighbourhood before I pulled the car in. I always did this, so that I could get a feel of the place. It could have been quite a pleasant avenue, but the trees had been pruned to their necks and stood there naked of branch and greenery as if reluctant to grow. Empty beer cans and rotting paper were strewn around the pavements and many of the windows in the vast Victorian edifices were boarded up. Other windows were blocked up with sheets of galvanised tin. I kicked through the rubbish and I just glimpsed in the dim lighted rooms of a second-floor flat, round black faces of West Indian children pressed against the window.

I found the entrance of the alley to Tony's ground-floor flat. I passed the empty dustbins and shuddered at the smell. There were numerous waterstained cardboard boxes lying around. In the blackness I couldn't see a doorbell, so I banged on the door with my fist. It echoed through the night. I was shivering with damp. There were no lights on and I tried to peer through a window, but a tattered drape hung loosely across it. I thumped the door a second time, already knowing that nobody would answer. I retraced my steps, and with some relief returned to the security of my car. I had no choice but to wait till the morning.

I did not want to ask Tony into the drawing-room too obviously, so at break time I asked him if he could help me take down the badminton net. 'I'll help you Sal,' offered a chorus of voices from the snooker table.

'No thanks, I need someone tall and Tony is indisputably the tallest. Okay, now break's finished back into the schoolroom. Where's Sue?'

'She's upstairs looking after Spark Two as Gloria's gone into school to see a teacher during the break.'

'Right, then you're all going to have to be extra good on your own. Have you got some work?' Chorus of 'too much' as they filed, chattering, into the schoolroom.

Tony and I went into the garden. Only when winter was on us did I take down the badminton net – it would be put up again next spring.

'Can you undo that knot without getting up the tree?'

'Yeah,' and he spat. His face was filthy. That I could see it over his black skin was a tale in itself. His eyes were sunk deep into their sockets and the whites were bloodshot. His anorak was tatty and his jeans were only partially zipped up.

'So how are things going, Tony? Enjoying Spark? Better than school, isn't it?' He nodded as he stretched to take the string from round the tree.

'You know, always after a kid's been here a term I go and see his mum, just to let her know how you're getting on.' I waited quietly to see if he would comment. He didn't. 'So would you tell your mum, as I can't phone her, that I'll pop over later in the week. Does she work?' He was folding up the net with great precision. It was as if he hadn't heard me. 'I shall look forward to meeting her and, more important, being able to tell her how well you're progressing here.' He had folded the net and handed it to me. He turned and walked into the kitchen and back to the schoolroom as Gloria walked through the front door.

'I went across to see Freddy's maths teacher. He's playing up – he's bunked two lessons this week.'

'The maths teacher or Freddy,' I said wryly.

49

'And what's the matter with you?'

'I've just performed an interesting soliloquy. Don't worry about it. If you're going upstairs, can you ask Sue to see me before she goes back to her group.'

'Surely, I'll send her down. Obviously, you don't want to talk about Freddy now?' She ascended the stairs two at a time not waiting for a reply. Sue caught me in the kitchen.

'How did it go? What did you learn?'

'Nothing. Absolutely nothing. He never even opened his mouth, well, only to spit.'

'So where do we go from here?' she asked.

'I'm not sure, to tell the truth. Let me get his file out, meanwhile you'd better go and see to your lot.'

His file told me little except that there was no father. A suspected boyfriend living with his mother, who could neither read nor write, and five younger siblings. So where had the entire family been last night? I turned a page and learnt about his primary school attendance and that he had been involved in petty crime from the age of eight. He must have a social worker then, I thought, but no one was listed. I closed the drawing-room door and locked it, a very rare occurrence. I looked up his address again, and then found the number of the social services in that area and rang.

They took what seemed like hours to answer and, even then, the duty officer seemed to begrudge the interruption. Yes, indeed, that family was well known to them, but she personally was not involved. Could I hold on and she'd put me through to the right office? 'Can I help you?' came the second voice. Yes she knew the family by name and reputation, but she personally wasn't involved. 'Could you put me through to someone who is involved please?' I said grumpily. There was a long wait and much clicking of the phone and then the same voice came back 'Hello, I'm sorry, the social worker who deals with that family is off duty – she'll be in tomorrow.'

I unlocked the door and Nick was standing there – 'What are you doing home at lunch time?'

'They've cancelled games this afternoon because the pitches are waterlogged.'

'You lucky lad – I suppose they don't reimburse me any school fees? As far as I can see the more school fees I pay out, the less education you get.'

'Had a bad day then? Is that why your door was locked?'

'No – I was trying to get hold of a social worker. Nick, do you know the tall black boy in Spark One?'

'No.'

'Good. Then he won't know you! Could you do something for me this afternoon?'

'Within reason, I've got a lot of homework.'

'I want you to follow a kid for me.' Nick threw back his head and laughed.

'Mother, you've been watching too many thrillers on TV.'

'No, I'm quite serious. Here, this is the address I think he'll make for – well, anyway it's his home address. I want to know if he goes there and, if not, where he does go. Just follow him for an hour or so. Pretend you're a private detective. I'll call you down just before he leaves.' My youngest went upstairs shaking his head. She really is going insane, I could hear him say to himself.

Insane or not, at last I was getting some answers. Nick returned within an hour of starting his assignment and informed me that Tony returned to his home address, placed his school satchel in an empty dustbin, collected all the cardboard boxes in the alleyway and stacked them up like a pack of cards. Having made his house against the alley wall, he had gone to a fish and chip shop. I had suspected it, but now I was sure – Tony was homeless, but where was his family?

At midnight I tiptoed down the alley until I came to his cardboard home. He must have heard me because when I peered in he was staring straight up at me, fully awake.

'Hi Tony, aren't you freezing? I've got the car here. There's a bed made up for you at home. You'll be more comfortable and a lot warmer.' I turned away and went and sat in the car. Five minutes later, he crawled into the passenger seat. We didn't speak on the way back and as soon as we got in, I showed him the bath. Over hot chocolate I said very firmly 'Tony, I don't know what's happened and

51

you're right it's none of my business, but it's going to be somebody's business tomorrow other than me, because I'm under an obligation to inform either the police or the social services.' He clutched his mug with both hands drawing out all the heat.

'My mum's gone away with the boyfriend. Hackney somewhere – she said the boyfriend would write the address down but 'e never did.'

'What about your brothers and sisters?'

'She's taken them wiv 'er.'

'But why didn't you tell someone?'

'Wot, and get 'er into trouble? She's good, my mum.'

'I'm sure she is, but you should have let someone help you; if we couldn't, the social services would have. That's what they are there for.'

'My mum don't like the social workers. She says that they will break up the family. Can I have some more chocolate?' And he spat.

We kept Tony a week, while the police searched for the family. They never found them in Hackney, nor anywhere else. One afternoon after school Tony gleefully appeared. 'My mum's come home, she didn't like it with the boyfriend.'

'I always knew she'd come back,' he said, and spat from the car window as we turned into his avenue.

Chapter 6

It is a sad truth that it is easier to respond to and look after someone else's children than one's own. It is also a realistic truth that one's own children, on the whole, behave no better, no worse than other people's children. I had spent the whole morning pondering this on hearing that Christopher could well be expelled from Winchester College. Apparently he had arranged to go to a dance by coach some thirty miles away on Saturday night with his housemaster's approval. But then he had spent the week in the san with his injured leg and was now hobbling about on crutches, so matron rightly advised the housemaster that it was 'inappropriate' and the housemaster rightly told my stubborn son that he couldn't go and instead was told to catch up on some of the work he had missed. The child defied him. He was unable to take the school coach because of the ban by the housemaster, so with a friend they hired a taxi.

'A taxi!' I exploded to the housemaster. Who paid, that's what I wanted to know? It must have cost them a fortune, sixty miles there and back. I knew Christopher did not have that kind of money. I only gave him an allowance of twenty pounds a month and out of that he had to buy all his clothes.

'Dr Smith, unless the child's won on the horses, he hasn't got that sort of money.'

'No, I gather the other boy paid.' I remembered my son

telling me of a very rich boy who had a taxi account at Winchester.

'Oh, it must have been Ding Dong,' I said without thinking. There was a silence at the other end of the phone. Had I said something wrong?

'I think you mean Sean East,' was the acid reply.

'Well is he known by the lads as Ding Dong?'

Another silence and then, 'No, you mean Doo Da.' Doo Da – Ding Dong – it sounded like some cryptic melody to me.

'Sorry, yes that's the fellow. He's a year ahead of Christopher, isn't he? I met him last time I was down. Well, I'm delighted he paid for it,' I added with relief, and as I heard myself I realised that this was not the major issue. 'I'm so sorry Christopher's behaving so badly. I'm sure when he sees the headmaster, he'll realise how childish he's been and will be deeply contrite. You're quite right, such disobedience and deviousness is quite intolerable. Perhaps when he's seen the head you could ask him to ring me?' I did not have to wait long.

'Mother, I've been told to ring you. What's the matter?'

'What do you mean, what's the matter? You've defied your housemaster, broken the school rules, been sent to the headmaster and you have the gall to ask what's the matter?' I could hardly restrain my anger.

'Oh, that! The head just rapped me over the knuckles. I don't regret it. It was a marvellous evening.' I listened in dismay. I was quite dumbstruck. 'By the way, Mother, I saw a specialist yesterday and I've apparently torn a cartilage. They might have to operate.'

'On your brain or your knee?'

'I don't think you realise what this means. Not only no football this term, but no football next term and I've been chosen to play for the school First XI. It's terrible. You do realise this is happening to me in the prime of my life?' I dredged my depths for sympathy I didn't feel. How could he behave like this? Where was the sensitive, thoughtful boy that I had sent off to boarding school three years ago? What had happened? What had gone wrong?

I must have looked gloomy when I replaced the receiver

for Nick said, 'Don't worry, Mum, he'll be okay at eighteen.' He looked at me so solemnly, as if a death had occurred in the family, that I began to laugh. 'I'll tell you something else. If he gets expelled from Winchester, he could always join Spark.' My laughter ceased.

Half-term was upon us once again. Although I had a week's break from the Spark children, I had six other children in the house.

I had had the idea of Overseas Educational Services some years previously. It was inspired by two horrific stories, the first from Christopher, about a rich Indian boy at his school, whose parents felt that the British independent school education was the best in the world. At thirteen, he was sent to this strange country to fit into a totally different culture, not knowing a soul here. At half-term his parents arranged for him to stay in a hotel for its duration and gave him two hundred pounds to take himself out to the theatre and for any other entertainment he required. In fact the child stayed in his hotel room and watched television because he was too frightened and too lonely to venture out.

The second story was about two South American girls, aged fourteen, who were sent over here to start boarding at a convent. It had all been arranged in South America by letter, but somehow the lines between the parents and the convent became confused and, in fact, on their arrival the school was neither expecting them, nor had room for them; so they also, not speaking a word of English, were put in a hotel while the problem was sorted out by the relevant embassy.

It suddenly occurred to me that I was in an ideal situation to provide a service to fill such a need. After all, I had a large house geared to children, with a video, computer, snooker table, croquet and badminton in the garden and all the facilities to support and care for children from abroad who might need the warmth and fun of family life.

So I formed a company with two directors and myself, according myself the grand title of managing director, and brought out an appealing brochure in pale green and gold proclaiming my suitability for children to be entrusted into my hands. I offered, for a large fee, to meet their children at the airport, take them to their new school, buy their school uniform, have the little darlings home at half-terms and weekends, keep the parents informed of their well-being and progress, arrange private medical/dental treatment, organise holiday entertainments such as country visits and other cultural activities.

All profits were ploughed into the Project Spark charity, thus exempting us from any taxation. I felt a little like Robin Hood, taking from the rich and giving to the poor. Although the Inner London Education Authority paid for all the staff in Spark, they did not pay for the house bills, the minibus, the outings, the annual holidays. As well as running Spark every year I had to raise twelve thousand pounds from public funds.

With the initiation of Overseas Educational Services I halved the soul-destroying burden of raising money, but it did mean I worked equally as hard at half-terms as I did during the terms, if not more, for I was having to produce three meals a day for never fewer than eight people. The first boy who came to us aged thirteen was from Japan. His name was Masahide Kawamura. He was eventually to live with us for the next seven years.

Rumours were rife. The Metcalfe and Hargreaves reports had been published, supporting the new policy that school support centres established for disruptive pupils remain attached to the main school provision and not become a separate form of secondary education. This was a crushing blow for Spark, because we were recognised as an off-site unit, our house was just two hundred yards from the main school site. This was despite our children's spending a good fifty per cent of their time in school following their exam courses. I feared Spark was doomed. If ILEA withdrew their financial support I would have to close down. Damn, damn politics.

The absurd thing was that it was not so long since the divisional education officer was singing our praises in a national newspaper. It read 'Spark offers a combination of discipline and loving care. They are highly successful in reintegrating pupils into mainstream education and the kids seem to respond admirably in a home setting.' A fresh wave of bitterness flooded my soul. What would happen to these damaged children? They would be caught up in the ruthless procedures of bureaucracy, inappropriate and insensitive to the unloved. They would become further victims of their behaviour difficulties and learning deficiencies. As this torment churned round my brain, I heard the post arrive. Among the mail was an ILEA report on the future procedure for school support centres and by the time I reached page three, my dismay and fears for the future were confirmed. Under the title of 'Management', I read:

> The control of units serving several schools shall be through a Management Committee. The composition of this committee should reflect the concept of a consortium where the Heads (or representatives) remain responsible for their own pupils. Whether each Head or representative (or delegated senior member of staff) are members of the Management Committee will be a matter for Heads to decide. The Divisional Officer, the Divisional Inspector and the Divisional Educational Welfare Officer shall be represented on these committees. The teacher in charge of the support provision should also be a member and other persons might be invited, when appropriate, depending upon their involvement with the child. The functions of the Management Committee will include recommending staff to be appointed to the centre, having oversight of the progress of the programme, supporting the teachers working in it, adjudicating in cases of conflict or referral or return to school and in general determining the aims and methods of the programme. The Chairman of the Management Committee, who shall be a Head of one of the schools involved, shall be responsible for its organisation, for ensuring that it carries out its functions effectively and, where necessary, for taking ultimate responsibilities for resolving any sustained disagreement on a particular case and ensuring that firm links are made between the centre and the linked schools.
>
> Appointments to posts of teacher-in-charge will be made

following the recommendation of a committee which should contain representatives of the Centre Management Committee and the Governors of the secondary schools involved.

Spark had never seen a school governor in ten years. What would they know about choosing the 'right' person for this specialised teaching in this unique environment? How could we cope with all this management purifying and disinfecting efficiency, and what was it going to do to help my distressed kids? What was all this to do with my child, Project Spark, born from a passion to give understanding and love to the loveless.

I felt numb and unbelievably disillusioned. Many years before, as a teenager, I had believed that good would overcome evil, that love would devour hate, that truth would defeat dishonesty. In such innocence I had bounded from the protective environment of a convent boarding school and home, to help the meths drinkers and drug-addicts who peopled the late nineteen sixties. I had turned a deaf ear to my parents' and society's disapproval and for four years sat on a rat-infested, smelly bombsite trying to help the rejects and the so-called scum of our city. We had shared the same feelings of loneliness, of neglect, of not being wanted. The physical agony of constant hunger and cold had been rivalled only by the constant rejection we had received from our fellow men. I had clung like a vine to my beliefs and scratched at disillusionment, but I learnt that the instinct of survival was the only significant factor of life. To see to the survival of Spark, at that moment, was that same basic simple instinct.

A paradox of the present times is that management and technology, which on one hand can bridge many divisions, have at the same time been instrumental in bringing about a state of affairs where there are more divisions in the world than ever before. Mass communications present mass problems to mass people and individual man is denied. It is no wonder that people split into divisions and groups and splinters in an attempt to discover themselves and find identity. Machines behave, while people experience. Of all

58

the divisions that there seem to be – political, social, religious – perhaps there is only one real division that continues through the ages and this is the one that exists between the servants of the spirit and the priests of the organisations, between those who have a renewing vision and those who can only grasp sufficient of it to try and organise it. It is axiomatic that the older one grows, the more stable and responsible one becomes and the less idealistic, so consequently from being one who is inspired, one progresses to being the organiser, whose powerful tools serve the contemporary gods of effective planning and efficiency. Unfortunately, neither management nor efficiency alone can make a better society.

I sat alone in my bewilderment of thoughts. I felt grievously wounded. Why, oh why, did they have to slur and axe the very goodness of life? Why, oh why, did they have to change what appeared to be working so successfully? My anger gave way to self-pity as I remembered the selflessness, the great life's-work I had promised Jake. The tears flowed as the tide of life drowned all courage.

After half-term the complaints came pouring in. First, it was Riki who had now returned home, who was falling back into his old habits. I discovered he had not attended a science lesson and then when he left Spark one morning for a maths lesson in school, he was seen with a friend disappearing in the opposite direction into town. Immediately I rang his mother, who was quick to inform me that he had been a changed boy over half-term, so charming and co-operative. She said she would have words with him and I said that he would be spending double the time here if he continued to bunk off. This was followed by a phone call from school complaining that Emily was always late for her lessons.

'Count your blessings!' I exalted unsympathetically to the angry teacher. 'If that's your only complaint about her, you're doing well.'

'Well, no, actually, there's more. Yesterday she walked out of my lesson. She picked up her things and just walked out.'

'Yes, it seems to be the trend at the moment.' There was a silence of disbelief.

'Well, what are you going to do about it?' the angry voice came back. I was tired and short-tempered.

'I'm not going to do anything. She's never walked out on us and when she does I will deal with it. Meanwhile, she's walked out on you, so you deal with it. I will see that she's at your next lesson on time. Good luck!' Yet another teacher who will never speak to me again, I thought, but I was too tired to care.

The next morning I was lying in bed, Nick having brought me a cup of tea. The phone went and it was Riki's mother.

'Oh Sally, Riki won't get up, and refuses to go to school. I don't know what to do with him.' I knew the feeling all too well: I didn't want to get up either.

'Have you asked him why he won't go to school?'

'He says he doesn't like the room he has to work in at school.'

'He says what?'

'I think you heard,' she miserably replied. Indeed I had.

'Let me speak to him. I've never heard such nonsense.' Riki came to the phone, but before he could open his mouth I said, 'Young man, I hear you won't go to school this morning because you don't like the classroom you have to sit in. I can assure you that if you don't get your precious backside into school this minute, you won't be sitting on it anywhere for a very long time. It'll be too sore. I will see you later this afternoon, when you can write a three-page essay for me on how you would decorate your classroom to your liking, and what luxury furnishings your sensitive little brain would choose.'

Riki came into school and later that day we collated a list of excuses for non-attendance: (1) didn't like the schoolroom; (2) took ageing parent to social security; (3) cat fell off eighteenth-floor balcony; (4) had to visit dying relative; (5) ill with hangover; (6) had to go and collect wages; (7) over-indulgent dentist took all day; (8) waited for bus all day; (9) suffered rigor mortis – unable to stand up; (10) dog peed on homework, so had to do it again.

Chapter 7

Christmasitis was already engulfing the shops, with six weeks still to go. Crocodile lines of cars queuing for parking places. Frenzied shoppers buying and babbling at twice the tempo. Dull human minds suddenly animated by the fervent desire to spend money. Booming production lines increasing the ambitious expansion plans of the profit-makers. I had taken the Spark One children shopping to buy decorations for the schoolroom. It was all too grotesque for me, weighed down as I was by the possible closure of Spark. On my return, I quietly disappeared with Dog up to the cemetery, as it was the closest walk at hand. I watched Dog squat on a tombstone. How odd life was – I could be killed tomorrow and find myself laid out in this same cemetery with my own dog relieving himself on my grave.

Feeling much better, I returned to my duties in Spark. I had hardly passed through the front door when Emily informed me she'd been sick at the end of the road that morning and that it was all red and would I like to go and inspect it. Before I could reply negatively, Piers interjected, 'She's always being sick in the mornings.' We all glanced knowingly at one another, but I decided that I didn't feel strong enough to tackle the subject of pregnancy – perhaps later in the week – so I changed the subject.

'Have you seen the new Spectrum Plus computer?'

'No, where?' Martin had joined us in the hall.

'For the moment I've put it in Christopher's room as he's not here.'

'Can we go and try it out?' asked Freddy.

'Yes, as long as you promise not to touch anything else in his room.'

A chorus of promises as they leapt up the stairs. I have an inherent dislike of machines, and computers were no exception. My dislike of them was based on my ignorance, therefore I found it quite astonishing that kids, who could hardly read or write, were able to work such highly complex apparatus. Gloria was descending the stairs. 'Half my class are missing,' she grumbled amiably.

'Sorry, my fault, I told them about the new computer.'

'Is Martin with them?'

'Yes.'

'He's on shopping for lunch. By the way, Gerry says the bike has another puncture.'

'Then Martin will have to walk to the shops won't he? And Gerry will have to mend the puncture if he was the last one to use it.'

The unofficial strikes by the teachers were becoming the norm. The National Union of Teachers at our local comprehensive decided to take action against the ILEA because they had failed to support their anti-racial policy at a school in the East End of London. Personally, I wondered why our children bothered to go to school at all when their education was being messed around so much. Whatever, I was determined that Spark remain open and made it quite clear to my teachers that I should respect their choice of action, but that our doors would not be closed. Hence, I found myself one morning in the Spark One schoolroom teaching English. I had taken the easy way out and set them an essay, even though I was aware that Marcus, an eleven-year-old Irish-born scamp, was not particularly well-endowed with the pen. Perhaps that was the reason he made no effort.

'What's the problem, Marcus?' I asked, having watched him fidget about for the last two minutes.

'Don't want to write an essay.'

'Oh, come on, it's not so hard. I'll help you.' I put my hand on his shoulder to encourage him to sit still, when he suddenly turned and with his clenched fist hit my arm away. His face looked as if he had blown a fuse, as if a volcano had erupted deep from his belly. His expression was of perfect hate.

'Don't you touch me you f——.' My heart seemed to stop for a moment. What my face registered I couldn't be sure – whether it was anger or violence, but the fiend that lurked within me released itself like a gigantic explosion and within less than a second I had cuffed him across his ear. It was quite wrong. It was as wrong as it was instinctive. I shuddered, scandalised. I wanted to say something, but nothing came. I felt bad inside. All this because I had wanted him to write an essay, and he had not wanted me to see how poor his skill was. Marcus was white, his teeth clenched, like his hands, his tight lips almost a blue colour, his eyes screwed up like two little currants, brimming with tears.

'You just wait, my dad will get you for that,' he whispered, but loud enough for all to hear. The other children were cringing collectively as one does if one encounters an unexpected force. I found my voice.

'Marcus, I'm sorry. I shouldn't have done that.'

'You'll regret it,' he muttered. His soft Irish colouring had returned to his cheeks.

'I do already. I'm sorry. It's done, I can't take it back.'

'Wait till I tell my dad.' This time it was said in a loud, threatening manner.

'Wot will your dad do?' Someone was recovering fast.

'Yer wait and see,' Marcus replied cockily. I had now recovered.

'Okay, there's ten minutes to finish your essays. A Mars bar for the first one to fill the page.' I glanced at Marcus to see if he would bother to lift his pen. He did, but not to write. He leant back on his chair and twiddled his short copper curls round it, watching me, hating me.

'Yer better look under yer car every morning,' that soft Irish burr usually so gentle to the ear, sounded ominous.

'Now why should I do that?'

'What yer goin' to do, Marcus?' one of the children interrupted.

'Just yer wait and see.'

'Go on, why should Sal look under 'er car every morning?'

My blood ran cold. 'Come, come on, finish those essays,' I contrived. I thought about it very carefully before I said it. 'Marcus, why don't you write an essay on how to make a bomb? Doesn't have to be more than a page, and keep the sentences short,' I encouraged. He looked at me and then slowly opened his writing book and began to write.

In the lunch hour I raced round to school to seek out the head of the chemistry department. He was an intensely serious man of few words. He read Marcus's sheet of paper. 'Can't spell, can he?'

'At this point in time I'm not interested in his spelling. It's the contents that worry me.' He read to the end.

'You should be Sally; that is a detailed and correct method of making an unsophisticated bomb.'

'Oh no! I really will have to look under my car every morning,' I groaned.

'Have you got problems?' He handed me back Marcus's masterpiece.

'Yes, I think you could say that,' I acknowledged. Fortunately I never did find a bomb under my car and, believe me, every morning I looked for one. Some years later I heard Marcus was in prison for inflicting grievous bodily harm. Every day one heard stories of violence.

I heard of a colleague, an educational welfare officer in Pimlico, who was making a late visit to a family at six in the evening when she encountered a group of teenage boys on the estate. It was well lit and she stepped aside to let them pass, as one of them drew out a gun and pointed it at her chest. She put her hands in the air while they went through her handbag and, having taken everything of value, they ran away. Another incident in the week was when an eleven-year-old boy attacked his teacher in the classroom at our local comprehensive.

Disruptive behaviour and delinquency in the young are not new, but this daily violence is becoming all too common. In Project Spark we have coped with many problems: dumb insolence, bullying, swearing, racial prejudice, smoking, lateness, truancy, and 'forgery' to conceal it. But I have noticed in the last few years the problems we have had to deal with have become far more serious – theft, wilful damage to property, shoplifting and assault. Last summer, an argument occurred over a game of snooker in the hall, when David threatened to hit his opponent, Joe, with a cue. Joe pulled a knife. I separated the two boys, but later David was found with a boiling kettle, which he intended to throw over Joe. The following morning before school, David with two other boys (not from Spark) laid in wait for Joe and a fight started. In the same week David was caught turning on the hot plate, while another Spark boy was cleaning the cooker after lunch. When reprimanded, he would not accept this was potentially dangerous, nor that any of the other incidents was wrong or in any way his fault. Following this episode his distraught mother telephoned to inform me that he had thrown a kitchen knife at his elder brother; because of his behaviour problems she was on the verge of a nervous breakdown.

David was now determined to get his revenge on Joe and had been observed on the train home threatening Joe's younger brother. It was quite clear to all the staff in Spark, and his mother, that this boy was extremely sick and in need of specialised help before he hurt somebody else or damaged himself. I asked the educational psychologist to come and see him immediately, impressing upon him the urgency of the matter. He came the next day and interviewed David for two hours, at the end of which he informed me that he couldn't help him without involving the father, who had no communication with the family and had always refused to accept that there was anything wrong. The educational psychologist suggested that if I took no further action David would soon be in trouble with the police and therefore he would no longer be my responsibility. I informed him of our caring and preventative philosophy and showed him the door.

Immediately I contacted the department of child psychiatry at the Royal Free Hospital and after some weeks had elapsed we were given an appointment. David, his mother and I were there for a whole morning, the outcome being that the two child psychiatrists informed us that they didn't feel they could help. They implied that he was quite unsuitable for their adolescent unit at the hospital, and when David's mother asked for psychiatric help for her son in outpatients, they said they didn't feel that was necessary either because he had such a good relationship with the staff at Spark. Now it was our turn to be shown the door!

In desperation, I contacted Camden Assessment Centre, which by chance was two hundred yards from where David lived. They agreed they had a vacancy for a boy, but couldn't take him because he wasn't under a social worker (I was educational welfare officer only). So I rang the social services, who asked me to submit a profile on the boy. I wrote it that morning and delivered it by hand that afternoon. A week later the senior social worker telephoned to inform us that they were only dealing with emergencies as they were on strike. Apparently David was not an emergency, despite his erratic and violent behaviour. She went on to add that because they were so short staffed, it would be unlikely that they would be able to allocate a social worker for four months. Camden Assessment Centre were very sorry they couldn't help, especially as they had a vacancy and that he lived just down the road, but they did suggest we referred him for assessment and some positive guidance to an educational psychologist. Full circle!

David did stay with us till he left school at sixteen, and we did contain him in Spark, but because of lack of 'co-operation', or is the word 'responsibility', better known as passing the buck, or perhaps it's bureaucracy gone mad, David was given no specialised help to treat his apparent illness.

Emily was causing further problems. I had had my tête-à-tête and she assured me she could not possibly be pregnant as she had been on the pill for the last year.

'But you're only fifteen,' I exclaimed in horror. 'Does your mother know?'

'Of course she do, Sal. It was her who made me go on it.'

'Well then, if you are being sick I think you ought to go and see your doctor. The pill you're on might be unsuitable for you.' We didn't refer to the subject again until the morning when her mother rang me over breakfast to say she hadn't been well last week, in fact she really hadn't been well for some weeks, but she was sending her in today. She obligingly drifted in at eleven o'clock.

'Who do you think you are? The patron saint of truants?' She shrugged her shoulders and made a point of turning her back on me.

'You rude little brat, you look at me when I'm talking to you.' I swung her round with both my arms grasping her shoulders.

'What yer doing?' she demanded indignantly.

'Forcing you to look at me. I'm not surprised you don't recognise force. No one's forced you to do anything ever, have they? Now why are you so late?'

'Had to wait for my Nan to come home, so the dog wouldn't eat the wires,' she replied sulkily, with tears in her eyes.

'Well you'll have to miss your lunch hour and catch up on the work you've missed.'

'Can't, meeting my dad at half past twelve.'

'I don't care whether you've arranged to meet the Prince and Princess of Wales because you're not going to. You're staying here and you're not going anywhere today.' As I walked down the stairs I heard the furniture being thrown round the room. I hoped Gloria had taken cover.

Dog was at the bottom wagging his tail. I stroked his broad head. 'Yes, I need some fresh air, too. Come on, let's get your lead.' It was snowing as we headed for the cemetery, which was now becoming our regular hunting ground. No one was to be seen until I spied earth flying through the air every ten seconds. I went to investigate. I found myself looking down into a large hole at the bottom of which was a gravedigger and spade. 'Bit cold for that isn't it?' I questioned. He looked up and nodded.

'They don't think of that when they drop dead.' He continued his rhythm of digging. I could not curb my curiosity.

'When's this going to be used then?'

'The bodies are coming in tomorrow. We can't leave them too long because of the weather.' I was confused.

'You mean the bodies or the graves?' He leant on his spade and stared at me.

'The graves. Of course in this weather it's not dangerous, but supposing this turned to rain. We prop the sides up with wood; if it rains heavily there could be a landslide and then what would the cortege do, if they arrived with the coffin and found no hole? I tell you what, they would have my scalp first.' The imagination boggled at the thought of it and I wanted to laugh, so changed the subject.

'It's a hell of a big hole for one coffin.'

'Cor luvaduck! This is a nine-footer. Three bodies going in here, ya know.'

'Of course.' How very stupid I was.

'I suppose it's cheaper to share a grave?'

'I don't know about that, and nor would they in their position like, but I can tell you the bigger the hole I dig, the more money I get, so it suits me. Any more questions like, or can I get on with my work?'

As I continued my walk with Dog and thought over the conversation I suddenly felt the urge for a bath.

Chapter 8

December was dominated by the NUT industrial action in support of their pay claim. They were on a four-day working week now. I was in school for a meeting about a Spark child, when I was informed that our local branch of the NUT had decided to use this month's allocation of half a day's unsustained strike action in a staggered series of short periods, which apparently made it quite impossible to keep the schools open for pupils aged eleven to fourteen. Since my fifth-years were on mock O-level leave, it virtually meant we could break up for the Christmas holidays. But, as always, I decided to keep Spark open in case any of my kids needed somewhere to go – most of them had only single parents who were out at work all day. Anyway, I had arranged to take them to the theatre the next week and there was the Christmas party. No, of course we had to stay open. I began to wonder if the teachers really believed these disruptive strikes were going to further their cause.

The house was like a morgue without the children. Dog and I padded from room to room half expecting a kid to leap out of a cupboard. The silence was eerie, not comfortable. I felt quite lost and was most relieved when the telephone rang. It was Christopher.

'Mother, I'm going into hospital tomorrow for that knee operation I told you about.'

'Good heavens! They give a lot of notice, don't they?'

'Sorry, but Sister only told me an hour ago.'

'Which hospital, and what's the name of the ward? Who's the surgeon? Who's doing it?'

There was a deliberate silence from the other end. I groaned in disbelief.

'Don't tell me you don't know.' I just couldn't credit him with being so stupid as not to have found out.

'No, I'm afraid I forgot to ask.'

'Well, Christopher, that's just great. Why would you expect me to want to ring up the hospital to find out if they've amputated your willie by mistake, or whether you'd died under the anaesthetic. You absolutely amaze me sometimes.'

'Calm down, Mum. My housemaster will know. Why don't you ring him?'

'Okay, I'll do that. When can I get hold of him when he's not teaching or busy with kids?'

'Try lunchtime – he's usually in his study directly after lunch.' So it was that I rang his housemaster.

'Dr Smith, Sally here. I wonder if you can enlighten me about Christopher's operation tomorrow?'

'Ah, yes. He's going into the san tonight and will go straight from there to hospital first thing tomorrow morning. He's very cheerful about it all and doesn't seem too worried.'

'Indeed, he's so casual that he doesn't even know which hospital he's going to,' I replied icily, and waited to be informed. It was silence that I recognised. 'Don't tell me, you don't know either? Does anybody know anything?'

'I'm terribly sorry, Sally,' he interjected hastily. 'I suggest you ring the san and talk to Sister as she has spoken to the specialist and has all the details.' I rang the san and spoke to a sane and sensible lady who gave me names, addresses, telephone numbers and all that I required.

I left the next day and took the Underground to Waterloo station. It was a bitterly cold evening and the brisk mile to the hospital in Winchester failed to warm me up. I found my way to the correct ward where I encountered the staff nurse and explained who I was.

'Ah yes, Christopher, he's still a little woozy from the anaesthetic, but you can go in,' and she pointed down

70

the dimly-lit corridor towards the private rooms. I peered through the little window and recognised his tousled hair, though his face was turned to the wall. There was no mistaking those canoe-like feet. I threw myself into the only armchair and waited. The last time I had been in this situation was when he had had his tonsils removed seven years before. He was a sweet child, mischievous but not capricious then. He was very mature and because of the absence of a male adult in the house, he had automatically taken on the role as protector of me and father of his younger brother, and this had influenced my decision to send him away to school.

He had been desperately homesick for the first year, and I wondered if this assumed carefree behaviour was a form of outlet for his suppressed pain. From experience I had learnt that superficial unconcern was the lot of energetic, over-active, impulsive children and it was children with a deep sense of pride that were most prone to lay on feigned nonchalance. As often as not they were kids like Christopher, who manifested real ability and at a young age achieved considerable success.

After all, Christopher had won an assisted place to Winchester College and, at the end of his first unhappy year, he was awarded the equivalent of the first form prize for his work. Also, he had won a place in the football, basketball and cricket teams. The second year his school record sloped off abruptly. I was firmly of the opinion now that my son's problem was that he had achieved success too easily, basically without effort. He had become accustomed to good marks, then when he was obliged suddenly to grapple with some serious work and make an effort, he did not actually comprehend what that involved, nor how he should go about it. He was a victim of his own lack of discipline.

He groaned, and I took his hand and caressed it. Perhaps I should never have sent him to boarding school. Perhaps all this concentrated activity on sport was a cover-up for his dejection and bewilderment. I put his hand lovingly to my cheek and he groaned again and turned his head towards me still in a deep sleep. I must have turned as pale as death and certainly as speechless, for there lying before me was

71

a tall young man but not with the features of Christopher. He had the same hairstyle, indeed the same feet, but it wasn't my son. Quickly I dropped to my knees to below the level of the bed so that he couldn't see me, for I did not want this boy to suffer nightmares of wondering who that strange, unknown, middle-aged woman plying him with love and caresses, was.

Very humbly I crawled from his room on my knees – what for heaven's sake would his parents have thought if they had come in? The staff nurse was staring down at me astonished.

'Er – dropped a button off my coat,' I muttered, rising to my feet. 'Where's Christopher exactly?' She pointed to the room next to where I had just spent the last hour. Christopher was sitting up being sick. When he finally stopped, he said cheerfully enough, 'Great to see you, Mother, jolly kind of you to come down. I was expecting you over an hour ago . . .' It was all too embarrassing to explain.

Gerry was in care. He lived with eleven other children in a large Victorian house run by the social services. Twice a year I was invited to their review meeting, where anybody and everybody came together to discuss the boy's progress or lack of it. It must have been most encouraging to him to see so many, so interested. There would be present up to six members of staff, his social worker, the senior social worker to the social worker, the educational welfare officer, the senior educational welfare officer to the educational welfare officer, me (the Spark educational welfare officer), the probation officer, the juvenile bureau officer, his tutor, his head of house and the head of pastoral care. Sixteen people would spend the whole evening rattling cups of coffee, airing their views about a child they rarely saw, some never having even met him. These were the most monotonous, ineffective evenings I spent, and when finally the staff insisted that Gerry should be present so that he didn't feel we were talking unpleasantnesses behind his back, which of course we were as this was the only fun of the evening, all possibility of any entertainment was extinguished and nothing was ever accomplished.

It was Freddy, always active on the grapevine, who brought the news:

''Ave yer 'eard Sal?' he exclaimed breathlessly one morning as he burst through the kitchen door.

'No, Freddy, tell me.' I was giving Dog his breakfast biscuits.

'Gerry! He's in big trouble.'

'Now you come to mention it, he hasn't come in this morning.'

''E won't be coming 'ere again Sal.' Freddy was enjoying his exclusive knowledge.

'What makes you say that?' I asked.

''Cause he's run away.'

'And where does your information come from?' I fed the cats their breakfast biscuits. Freddy tapped the side of his nose in a gesture of cheerful gravity.

'Can't tell yer that, can I? I don't snitch.' His new self-importance gave him a startling, distinct precociousness. I knew not to insist on further information and that if there was any truth in his declaration I would sooner or later hear. It was sooner rather than later. The children's home was on the phone to me before the cats had finished their breakfast.

'I'm afraid Gerry won't be in this morning,' said a voice stiffly.

'Is he ill?'

'No, he's beaten up a boy so badly that he's now in intensive care and Gerry's on the run.' Inside I froze, but outwardly appeared sympathetic, not to mention curious.

'When did this happen?'

'This morning.' How did Freddy know of this crisis then? My mind was trying to recollect exactly what Freddy said.

'How bad is the injured lad?'

'The doctors say he's got a fractured skull. We found the weapon. An iron bar. It was a brutal attack. I think the police will be round to see you later in the morning.'

'I don't know why, he's not hiding under my bed,' I replied dryly, and this curtailed any further conversation. I was baffled. Gerry was a timid lad, who spoke little. Usually he was wrapped in that inner dream that protected him from

73

realities too painful to face. He had a gentle, silent approach to life that gave him an air of solemn mystery. Emily summed him up succinctly: 'He don't really belong to this world.' Certainly, it was beyond my wildest imagination that he could pick up an iron bar and half kill another kid.

He was not of a naturally lively disposition, but nor was he an introvert. He was certainly not the hot-blooded type. I couldn't make sense of any of it, as I told the police later in the morning. As the days passed and the lad in hospital recovered, there was no news of Gerry. He had gone to ground. I wandered aimlessly here and there, quite wretched with concern. By the end of the week, he was still missing and I was convinced he was being hidden, for cold or hunger would have forced him into the open. Both the children's home and the police agreed with this analysis and suggested that I had words with his friends.

'He was a loner. He wasn't particular mates with anyone special, but I'll have a go.' I decided on a group session rather than individual interrogation, so over lunch on the Friday I initiated a conversation with Gloria for all to hear.

'If Gerry isn't found soon I shall start fearing the worst.'

'You don't think he's dead?' Gloria looked suitably horrified.

'I just don't know what to think. I'm sick with fear for him.'

'Ah, Sal, Gerry'll be okay.' Piers's eyes were singularly piercing.

'If he's sleeping out in this cold he'll die of hypothermia, and apparently he left without any money so he can't be in a bed and breakfast.' Freddy and Piers glanced briefly at one another, exchanging some secret. I wasn't meant to see it, but such vigilance came from years of habit. I let the subject drop and later in the afternoon as the two were leaving I called them into my room. It was time for the direct approach and a little bit of bluffing.

'Right you two. You're in trouble and we've got to find a way out.' They wriggled in their chairs uneasily, but remained mute.

'The police have been round and informed me that they are convinced that Gerry's friends are aiding and abetting him in hiding. I know this to be true. I know you see it as helping out a mate, but you can't go on feeding him for ever.' They sat stonefaced, but not denying anything I said. My guess had been accurate.

'Look, you guys, it's better to sort the problem out. It's never as bad as it looks.'

'He thinks 'e'll be sent away,' Freddy declared.

'Well, if he is, we'll fight it. I will do everything in my power to help him. You know that.'

'Wot if yer can't stop 'em?'

'Stop them doing what?'

'Taking 'im away.'

'I can't predict what the courts will decide, but the fact is he has caused serious injury to a kid.'

'Weren't his fault, Sal.'

'Until I've spoken to Gerry and heard his story I'm not prepared to comment, so I think the best thing all round is for you to take me to him.' Piers dropped his head, so as not to look at me. Freddy stared glumly at Dog whose nose was perched on his right foot. I pushed my chair back and advanced towards them, appealing to their good sense. 'Come on, Gerry needs help, let's go and help him.' In the car, I saw that every now and then they stole a curious look at my face, as if to make sure that I was not deceiving them. They directed me for some miles and then we halted before a large, squalid house. It was in a disreputable street where faded gentility had submitted to the struggle of poverty. I followed the boys down some stone steps past mounds of nettles and dockweed.

'In 'ere,' Piers pointed through a low, arched door balancing on one hinge at an angle. I followed the two boys into a decaying room. There was a mattress on the floor, a petrol drum with a dirty plate on it, endless discarded beer cans thrown at random round the place. It was bitterly cold and I could hear the wind moan through the hollow chimney, but it was the smell of excrement that caused me to put a handkerchief to my face. From the shadows, the dirty figure of Gerry lurched into view.

'We brought Sal,' Freddy explained weakly.

He stood there, his head hung, his hungry eyes darting

from Freddy to Piers to me. Suddenly he cried out, but in a muffled, subdued manner, as if in fear of raising his voice, afraid that his words would be lost in the millions of rents and blotches on the disfigured walls. I thrust myself forward with open arms and he fell upon my breast sobbing and I wrapped my arms around him. It was like a still-life, nobody moved in that desperate place. What reflections the boys clung to I do not know, as the bony child in my arms struggled to compose himself against the tide of desolation. No words were ever spoken between us in that deplorable house again. Gently, with my arms round Gerry's shoulders, I led the boys out. It had just begun to snow.

The children's home agreed that he could stay with us until the court case, the main reason being they did not want Gerry present when the injured lad returned from hospital. Gerry had confided in me that this boy was the first person he had ever felt any tender attachment towards. They had had a physical relationship, unbeknown to anyone. Then one morning Gerry had found his lover in bed with a member of staff. He had gone out into the yard, picked up an iron bar and smashed it over the child's head. As far as I was concerned, he had hit the wrong person.

I watched the boy deteriorate beneath the pressure of his hidden grief. He could not disengage his mind from the brooding guilt that sank deep into his soul. He contended with anxiety and depression alternately staring for hours out of the window or sitting still and motionless in his room, whiling away the interminable days before he was called to Juvenile Court. I so desperately wanted to restore his peace of mind as I heard him cry into his pillow at night, but there was nothing more that I could do. I knew he would be sent away. He knew he would be sent away. Truly there was nothing more I could do.

Chapter 9

Masahide, now aged fourteen, from Japan, arrived to spend the Christmas holidays with us from his boarding school in Lyme Regis. Christopher came out of hospital and the day after, came home for the vacation, caused his usual disruption and then crutched away again to some party in the country, leaving a message requesting me to organise an appointment with the local GP to have his stitches taken out.

Perhaps he thought better of being in the house when his school report arrived. His perceptive tutor wrote 'Chris does not wish to be thought of as an intellect and in case one might mistake him for one, expresses his ideas on serious subjects in only moderately legible schoolboy patois. He is a great deal less careful than he ought to be. His English style is breezy, he has a gift for narrative and could become a successful popular novelist, and is never less than readable on any subject except one requiring careful distinctions. He is immensely likeable – too likeable for his own good! He should now take his work more seriously.' God bless the man, whoever he is – I saluted him for being able to see that my son's strength of character was sadly his weakness.

I went upstairs and found Nick in bed with gloves on. 'Honestly, Nick, the central heating is on. It can't be that cold. In fact if you bothered to get up and look out of the window, you would see the snow has melted.'

'I'm not wearing gloves because I'm cold,' he answered

without looking up from the paperback that he was engrossed in.

'Then why are you wearing gloves in bed?'

'Well, I've bought Jan and Stefan' – his two eldest brothers and my two eldest stepsons – 'these books for Christmas presents, but I wanted to read them first and didn't want to put dirty fingerprints over them, so I'm wearing gloves to keep them clean.'

'Why not just wash your hands like other people?' I muttered.

'Yes, that was another alternative,' he admitted.

Christmas is not my favourite time of the year. Sadly, the commercial emphasis has overtaken the spiritual significance. But what do children care of that? They merrily applaud the fun and anticipate the pleasures of tomorrow. Last year's Christmas party had been a significant turning-point in Freddy's life. It was the last day of term. I had bought lager and lemonade, pizzas, cakes, ice cream and wine for the teachers. I could hear laughter in the schoolrooms as the kids put the final touches to the Christmas decorations. For me it was more than the last day of term, it was the end of another year in Spark. I hoped we had touched many hearts, but could not guarantee we had reached even one.

What of Spark in the future? My door was thrust open and then came the forgotten knock and Freddy's crooked urchin grin. He had settled well after the initial shock of realising that we actually cared about him. His eyes were bright with excitement. He was a burst of sunlight on my doubts. I felt the high-voltage charge across the room. 'We've finished, but you can't come in yet – well – not until you've opened this.' Very carefully, but with great excitement and pride, from behind his back he thrust out a package wrapped in tatty, crinkled Christmas paper. 'For you.' I stared in surprise. He tilted his head, watched me but didn't speak.

It was obvious that it was a present for me but I hesitated. 'From you?' He nodded as I took it from him. Suddenly he took a step forward and threw his arms round me before rushing out of the room, leaving me staring at the parcel. From the weight and the shape I knew exactly what it was and in this upside-down world in which I found myself, my heart sank. Uncertain, hesitant, hoping from the bottom of my heart that it wasn't, I unwrapped my precious gift. It was a bottle of whisky. What could I say? I was unwilling to ask where he had pinched it from.

He had no mother; his father was out of work and never had enough money to buy Freddy any sweets, let alone whisky, and only a few days ago some of the kids had expressed their fears that he was shoplifting in Woolworths. I felt a shadow across my heart. I didn't want to spoil the day. I wrestled with my conscience. Did I have to have it out with him now, could it not wait till next term? The answer was simple enough, but the effort somehow defied the answer.

Slowly I walked into the boisterous laughter of the transformed schoolroom. Freddy sat watching my entrance intently, chin cupped in his hands. The kids must have been aware of my solemnity for the noise abated and they exchanged looks. I looked from one to another and cleared my throat to capture their attention. 'Okay, set up the turntable and let's start with musical chairs.' Whoopee! They were hopping, jumping and skipping to the howling music. I signalled Freddy to follow me. I don't know how long we sat there in my room staring at each other. It seemed for ever as I struggled to find the right words.

'Freddy, that's a very special gift you've given me.' He closed his eyes and grasped his hands together, as if to settle some inner aspect of himself.

'You really like it,' he beamed. I faltered for a second only.

'Of course I like it but . . . well . . . Freddy, you like it here in Spark don't you?'

'Oh yes,' he mouthed. 'I feel safe here,' he hurled the words at me, his eyes lighting up like a Roman candle.

'Do you know why you feel safe here?'

'Search me. I dunno.'

'You feel safe because you feel trusted. I trust you and you trust me.'

'So?'

'Well, Freddy, I think you're in a muddle and I want you

79

to trust me to help you sort it out.' His smile died and his face flipped into a frown.

'Yer trying to tell me somefink ain't you? Yer trying to tell me you don't want that bottle of whisky.'

'No Freddy, slow down. I think the idea of giving me a present – well – I'm deeply touched, but I have to ask you where it came from.'

'Don't matter where it come from do it?' he said chokingly, his brow furrowed.

'I'm afraid it does, Freddy. I can't accept stolen property.'

'Why not, it don't belong to anybody else. I haven't hurt anybody by taking it, nobody ain't going to miss it.' There were tears smarting in his eyes. I so wanted to open my floodgates of comfort and reassurance, but I knew I had to man the guns.

'To steal – to take what doesn't belong to you is wrong.' Through his sobs he cried.

'But Sal, you've always told us it's the thought that counts.'

I tried to say something, but nothing came. Freddy bent double in misery, his eyes wild and wide, tears pouring down his cheeks, both hands pressed over his lips as if to stifle an explosion. My mind was racing to find words, but I couldn't get into gear. I couldn't find a starting point from which I could explain – the words just didn't fit together in any kind of reasonable pattern. I went to my chest of drawers and found a hankie and shoved it under his nose.

'Come on, blow it and go and get me a glass. I could do with a drink.' One can afford to be generous when one's in the elevated position of command, however wrong it might be.

This Christmas was full of change. Sue, after three years, had left to enhance her career, and a new teacher from the school was taking over Spark One. I encouraged my teachers to move on after a couple of years, for the work here among our children was intensive and very exhausting. So when Gloria gave in her notice, after two years with us, I was not altogether surprised. As the New Year was celebrated I had never longed so ardently for rural fresh air, nor pined

80

so long for open country. I knew there was change in the air, I could smell it.

It all happened quite simply. There was no warning, no letter, no discussions and, on the first day of the spring term, no teacher and no children. I phoned the school to find out what was happening, and was stunned to be told that Spark One had been closed. I stormed round to the school to see the headmaster. A sense of loss had descended upon me, together with not quite believing nor fully understanding just who I had lost or why I had lost them. Without looking me in the face as he busied himself with papers on his desk, he explained that it was a decision made at County Hall and that I surely must have been prepared for it, having been informed of the new policies for disruptive children.

'But what's going to happen to my kids?' I wailed.

'We have just moved your younger unit from your house into a schoolroom here; they'll have your new teacher and you'll keep Spark Two and nothing will be different.' I couldn't believe the ignorance of the man – 'Nothing will be different.'

The magic of Spark was that it was a home, not an institution. Rage, like a flame consuming my whole body, leapt through my veins, followed by an aching hunger for my children, whom I had failed to protect, the final and deepest humiliation. I heard his ice-cold voice say, 'If you want to protest you can take it up with the divisional officer, but I fear you'll be wasting your time.' I walked past him, ignoring his existence and in blind grief strode home shaking with uncontrollable anger.

I spent all day ringing the powers-that-be at County Hall, but I was never allowed past the previously elected secretaries. I was quite convinced that there was a conspired blackout, and as the days passed and my messages never got through, nor my letters ever answered, my persecution complex descended like a silent rebuke on my unworthy shoulders. If only Spark had had enough money to employ its own teachers. If only the previous headmaster hadn't resigned, for he would have had none of this. If only . . . If only . . . If only . . . it was almost as if I had become infatuated by my own recriminations; night and day, a constant ruthless torment of self-flagellation. It was not helped by the children themselves, often turning up in their lesson-times or before school, asking if they could come back to Spark here. They were as heartbroken as I was, which gave me no satisfaction in my desolation. In fact, the truth was that I loved more intensely because I had lost so much.

At the beginning of every year, as director of Project Spark, one of my responsibilities was to write the annual report. This was a summary of the previous year – what we had done with the children, where we had taken them for their holidays, the results of their exams and attendance; and by law we had to show the annual accounts. Once printed, they would be sent to all those who had financially contributed to the Project over the years and to the Charity Commissioners. I hibernated in the drawing-room behind locked doors so as not to be disturbed. My inherent dislike of bureaucracy helped reinforce my antagonism for this duty. I dreaded it every year, but especially now; to have to write an informative and ecstatic report which would enthuse our sponsors to put pen to chequebook, when ILEA had cut the Project in half, and as yet had not agreed to providing Spark Two with a full-time teacher, made my task no less easy.

It was a drastic beginning of term. The removal of Spark One from the house affected everybody and the older children in Spark Two who had rarely mixed with the younger members, except at celebrations, were as devastated as I was. They also were having to cope with a supply teacher now that the lovely Gloria had left, and a new teacher, however brilliant, would be resented, for any change meant insecurity for our kind of child.

Also there had been a cataclysm in Spark. It was initiated at the end of last term when I put Emily in the bathroom for the afternoon for being rude. She refused to attend at the beginning of this term and sent some obscene messages via the other kids – one of them being that she wasn't coming to this f——house again! I waited a few days and then heard down the grapevine that a close relative of hers had died suddenly and she now wasn't in school. I decided to pre-empt further hostilities, so on the following Sunday evening I rang her mother and suggested she brought in

Emily on Monday morning before she went to work – after all, she had never visited Spark and surely she would like to see the environment that her daughter worked in. The mother agreed, but it wasn't with total confidence that the teacher and I waited for them at nine next morning. So many times parents had agreed and then without a word not turned up. How wrong I was! Mother and child arrived exactly on time and we sat in the drawing-room over mugs of coffee baring our souls to one another, while sullen child scowled perversely. The more we talked, the more we agreed, and the more aggravated and tight-lipped Emily became until she could not bear our affability any longer and exploded:

'I don't care wot either of yer say – I'm not coming back 'ere.' Her diminutive, pretty mother turned on her.

'Oh yes, you will, my girl. They won't have you in school 'cause you're too much trouble, and I won't have you at 'ome when I'm out at work. So make up your mind to it, you're coming back here.'

'She'll pick on me,' the child nodded towards me.

'Indeed I will,' I cheerfully replied. 'If you give me trouble I'll give you trouble. You should know the rules by now. Work hard, behave yourself and you will be rewarded.'

'How would you reward me then?' she asked sulkily. I thought for a second.

'You want to learn needlework don't you?'

'Yeah, you know I do.'

'Well, if you complete all the work that is set and haven't been abusive during the week to us or teachers in school, we'll teach you to make your own clothes.' I could see that she didn't believe me. 'You keep your side of the bargain and I'll keep mine.'

A few days later I went into the local comprehensive and charmed the head of the needlework department and came away with an electric sewing machine and put it on the sideboard in our schoolroom. Emily saw it there, but made no mention of it until the end of the week, when she asked vociferously, 'When can I start making my clothes?'

'You're quite right. I've had no complaints; last two lessons this afternoon.' Today, the name of the game is charm, punctuality and a hundred per cent attendance. But for how long, I wondered.

It was Emily, now emboldened by good marks and flattery, who pranced into my room after school as I sat in my armchair in deep contemplation with Dog stretched out at my feet. She was a light, fluttering little figure, trendily dressed, with a wild far-off look in her eye. Without invitation she threw herself on to the sofa. Dog shifted positions and went over to her with his tail wagging, desiring affection.

'Tell me, Sal, do yer believe in God?' That was what I liked about Emily, I never did know what she was going to do or say next.

'Yes, do you?' She puckered her eyebrows.

'Well, Gran says I 'ave to and when we stay wiv 'er in the country we 'ave to go to church, so 'spose I do.'

'Going to church doesn't mean you have to believe in God.'

'Like I don't believe in school?'

'No Emily, the only reason you don't believe in school is you don't like being forced to go.'

'That's wot I mean. Gran forces me to go to church like.'

'Church is a symbol. It's a building. It's God's house where his followers can congregate in prayer and whatever.'

'Do yer pray?'

'Yes.'

'Why?' I glanced at her uneasily, but her youthful face looked steadily at mine.

'Well, I believe in God, as I've said, and prayer is talking to God. No point in believing in Him and not talking to Him,' I answered.

''Ow often do yer talk to 'im?'

'How often do I talk to you in the day, Emily? Like you, some days I communicate with Him more than others.'

''E don't misbehave like me, so yer don't 'ave to talk to 'im much.' I smiled.

'No, but I misbehave, so I have to talk to Him asking for help and His forgiveness.'

'Get away! Yer don't, do yer? When do yer misbehave? What do yer do?'

84

I really did not want to share my sins with Emily, so replied with somewhat diffident grace, 'Get angry with you kids when you swear. Anyway, what's prompted you to talk about God?' She bit her lower lip, reddened and thought and then in a kind of breathless whisper, she said:

'My best friend says yer can 'ave a baby without . . . well . . . yer know,' she winced in embarrassment, 'without a man.' I am not the sort of woman who is dumbfounded easily, but in this instance I was quite stupefied. It was a little time before I replied.

'Not to my knowledge, Emily,' I said firmly.

'My friend said she did.' Oh God! Did I have to go into the birds and the bees at this time of afternoon?

'I think your friend was having you on.'

'No she weren't; she said this lady gave birth to Jesus and 'ad never 'ad a man.' In relief I grinned with affection at Emily's comical confusion.

'Ah! I see now! Yes that's quite true. Our Lady, who was the mother of Jesus, was a virgin when she conceived her child. This was called a miracle and it hasn't happened to anyone since,' I asserted. 'She was especially chosen by God, you see.'

'Is that why yer believe in God?'

'No, not because of the Virgin Birth.'

'The wot . . .?'

'It's called the Virgin Birth because of her purity on the birthday.'

''Cause she 'adn't 'ad it off?'

'Yes, exactly. You've got it.' She rubbed Dog's tummy, who was now lying with paws in the air, paralytic with pleasure. She was digesting this latest information when Nick came in from school. Dog rolled over and greeted him vociferously.

'Hello, Emily,' he said warmly, not realising she was at the height of religious debate, giddy with a thousand and one questions. 'How's the world treating you?'

'Okay. Do yer believe in God, Nick?' Nick, for an instant only, was struck speechless, then without flinching he replied, 'Yes.' He gave me an imploring glance.

'Why?' she asked in her normally aggressive manner. I

watched the two teenagers eye one another. This was not the intimate type of question that cemented good relationships. His disparagement was final.

'Actually, Emily, I don't think it's any of your business. It's between me and my God. I'm going to make some tea.' Having disentangled himself, he shuffled out, leaving poor Emily turning red.

'Who does he think 'e is?' she said, half angry, half sorry perhaps.

'It's a very personal question.'

'Anyone would think I'd asked 'ow often 'e'd kissed 'is girlfriend.'

'Don't worry about it and just for the record, he hasn't got a girlfriend.'

'I can see that. 'E should get one quick and then 'e wouldn't be so bloody uptight.'

Chapter 10

Spark was rampant with illness. The teacher was in bed and Emily nobly arrived with heavy cold and sore throat and went home. One Spark lad was sick, so with white face departed and then a call came from Riki to say that he had been unable to make the journey in, because he had had too much chilli-con-carne the previous night and now had the runs. So I decided to take the remainder of the children out for the morning to the London Museum. In the afternoon I had to go into the local school for a meeting. As I was passing through the vestibule where children were forbidden to congregate, I observed a teacher shooing off a group of sixth-formers. They pretended they hadn't heard and turned their backs on her and pointedly held their ground. The teacher, realising they were not about to recognise her authority, rushed down the corridor to find the deputy head and both returned to deal with the situation. The sixth-formers appeared not to notice his vocal remonstrations and continued chatting among themselves, determinedly not shifting. The second deputy head, after renewed clamours to leave, turned to the teacher and shrugged his shoulders. 'Well, they're not doing any harm here,' and marched back to his study. I felt outraged by the senior master's attempt at discipline and final resignation of authority, and equally outraged by these seventeen-year-olds who had no respect for either the rules or their elders. It was very depressing and I deeply resented this role I was frequently having to play as trustee of the past and custodian of the present. So I also did nothing and continued to my meeting.

It was held in the deputy head's office, after I had complained that the school was not passing on the information to us when the strikes were being called. He presented a very gloomy picture. It was apparently impossible to cover for those teachers who took industrial action and approximately a hundred children were being sent home each day. Positions and resignations were not being filled. Half-term was in two and a half weeks and so far this term there was no head of the geography department and the assistant deputy head was heavily pregnant and near collapse. I pointed out that my Spark children had had only three maths lessons in school in six weeks this term because the teacher hadn't been there, or he'd been late and though he turned up last week, because there were only three pupils present he was not prepared to teach them, so they sat through his lesson doing nothing. I demanded from the deputy head what procedure I should follow to make a formal complaint, to which he replied that I shouldn't waste my time, all the schools were in similar chaos and that the future was very bleak, as the ILEA were cutting eighty million pounds off the educational system next year.

After the meeting had finished I opened up one of the national papers and read that a survey to record the ethnic origins of all ILEA employees was launched by the Authority that week. I was dumbfounded. Here they were about to cut back on eighty million pounds from the education of children and yet were spending money to record the ethnic origins of their employees. The world had gone mad! Priorities were upside down. Was there anybody left in this world with any common sense apart from me?

On my next visit into school for a meeting, I was inundated with complaints about my children. One of them had been caught procuring money from younger boys with threatening and menacing behaviour, and with discreet probing I discovered he had organised and was running a gambling syndicate. Within seconds of discovering all this, the head of another house drew me aside to inform me that our latest Spark candidate, Thomas, who only arrived the previous week, had turned up half an hour late for a maths lesson at which point the teacher refused to have him in the class. My little petal opened his big mouth and called him something very rude.

I agreed such behaviour was indefensible and that I would deal with the boy as soon as I caught up with him. As I was coming through the front door the telephone was ringing. This time it was the assistant deputy head informing me that the same lad had behaved intolerably in the art class and the teacher wasn't prepared to have him in her lessons any more. I proceeded to the schoolroom to find the child, only to be told that because of the staggered strikes he had been sent home – as had two of my other children. Within an hour a letter was sent out to the parents by the headmaster, saying that in line with recommendations from the NUT national executive, the NUT at his school had decided to take staggered action from the following Monday for two weeks up to half-term and that it was likely that groups would have to be sent home with no notice during this period.

I was getting the very strong impression, whether it be their fault or not, that my kids were virtually not getting any education at all. They really were having a traumatic time! I was convinced it was the lack of continuity and disruption by the teachers in school. It was very hard for two of my children who were school phobics. Over the last year I had had to cajole them gently to pass through the school gates, often I had to take them, and now just when we had got a routine going and they were making immense efforts to overcome their fears and get themselves into school for registration, they were sent home for the day. I caught one of them on his bike that morning.

'You should be in maths. What the hell are you doing out here?'

'We've been sent home, Sal.' He pulled up his cycle beside me.

'Then why haven't you gone home?' I demanded.

He hesitated. 'Well, Sal, it's my mum. She'll go mad. Yesterday, there weren't no teacher and she did her nut when I came home.'

'She'll do her nut if she knows you're wandering the streets. Come on, you'd better come back to Spark – it's too cold to wander the streets. At least it's warm there.'

'Say, Sal, would yer ring me mum and explain to 'er.'

'Yes, of course I will. Have you got her work number?'

'Nah, but we can look it up in the book.' He walked beside me, pushing his bike, a blond, curly-haired, freckle-faced imp. He was hoping to join the army when he left us in the summer, but he feared he was too small.

On our way in we met the Spark teacher who informed me that Emily, at home ill the previous day, was sitting on the school steps with her mates when she should have been in class or home in bed. Fortunately, her mother rang me to find out if the school was officially closing next week and I was able to tell her that her sick child had been seen holding court on the school steps. The mother was amazed as she'd left her at home in bed with a supply of medicines while she went to work. With teachers taking staggered twenty-minute strikes throughout the day, and groups of children being sent home at a moment's notice because there was nobody to cover for the strikes, it was quite impossible to know who was where, and for my sort of child, who desperately needed a framework of discipline and security, it was fatal.

I had Thomas, the lad who verbally abused his teacher, in my room this morning – he denied having been rude. I bawled him out and told him he wasn't going with the other children to the cinema to see *Rocky IV* that afternoon, and instead he would spend the time working with me in the schoolroom. He was very glum for the rest of the morning.

Wonders never cease! Thomas, who was due to have an English lesson in school before he came to me for the remainder of the afternoon, arrived to tell me that he'd been sent home because of the strike. The boy could have gone straight home with a reasonable excuse to have missed coming here to fulfil his punishment. These kids never ceased to surprise me. I sent him to do the work I set him for the afternoon, but rewarded his honesty by letting him leave three-quarters of an hour early. Another hump over!

90

I had often noticed a vital precondition for friendship between teacher and pupil were shared interests and aspirations, and I often went out of my way to ensure that I had not only researched the child's emotional and physical background before he arrived with us, but also his life-style. One didn't talk to a lad about Mozart's clarinet concerto if he listened only to heavy metal music. I wondered if he had been prepared to return to fulfil his punishment because I had had a long conversation about football, or was it just that being a new boy, he was not yet sure enough of me to disobey me?

By the end of the week, it was decided by the headmaster under pressure from the strikes, that school was to be closed for years one, two, three and four till half-term – the children this morning came in elated. I swear they won't be so elated after twenty days' holiday; boredom will have set in by the weekend. What of those poor parents who were working and not at home to look after and supervise their youngsters? Already I have had two phone calls asking me would I keep Spark open for their kids to come in as they've nowhere to go. This term, my children who were following a maths exam course have had only five maths lessons in school; that's less than one a week. It is quite preposterous.

Gloomily, I took Dog for his walk across the playing fields to the cemetery where I encountered my animated gravedigger. 'Bloody weather – it's neither one or other. I don't mind the sun and I don't mind the frost, but this dampness gets right through to my bones.' I stared depressed at his hole as he continued his monologue. 'You know the only thing to do on a day like this is sit at home by a fire with a glass of brandy. Still, it's good for business, this weather's knocking them off faster than I can dig their holes.'

I continued my walk feeling more damp and more depressed than ever before. Indeed I felt like a break, just to get away, perhaps drive over to a friend's for lunch or a glass of wine, perhaps even a brandy, in order to pour out all my anger and frustration at my inability to do anything to change the blighted system, or help these children, who were now suffering from it. Despite the ludicrous disparity in our years and our backgrounds, a deep empathy had sprung up between me and these children. For their part they had taken me into their confidence and prevailed upon me to accept them with all their problems and difficulties. However hopeless the situation was, I could not abandon them now, so, laying down my dreams of respite, I went home and opened up Spark, should anyone need somewhere to come for the day. At least *our* doors would remain open.

My mail was an interesting mixture. The first one I opened was from a convict in Gloucester Prison giving me his life story and telling me how wonderful I was. I only wish I felt it. This was followed by a Malawian, residing in Ethiopia, where he was working for the United Nations Economic Commission for Africa, asking about the possibility of arranging a guardian for his twelve-year-old son who was coming to school in England. It appeared that my company, Overseas Education Services, was becoming known! The third envelope contained some tickets for the theatre to which I was taking the Spark children, and finally there was a thank-you letter from Christopher's girlfriend for Sunday lunch which she had nibbled at because of her diet. I was delighted to receive it and discover that some of the young still hold to old-fashioned courtesy.

Assuming that no Spark children would attend today, I decided to get to grips with the upstairs toilet which smelled like a public convenience. A fatal decision for, having scrubbed the walls, I realised what it really needed was fresh paint. I searched the garage and found some white gloss which unfortunately was just what was needed, so reluctantly set to with brush and paint. I'm one of those people who invariably gets more paint on the floor than on the walls and spends more time picking hairs from the brush off the walls with my nails than painting. Whatever, it was my usual disaster of patches and streaks and I wished I had left it stinking like a French bog. Especially as it desperately needed a second coat which I couldn't now do till tomorrow. Meanwhile the cats had found the paintpot and glossy white paw marks crossed the landing and continued in a matching pattern down the stairs and through the hall. I decided life wasn't worth living, so I crawled into bed in my paint clothes, totally aware that I had no turpentine in the house, and wrote to the convict in very modest terms about my lack of achievements. I was reminded of Martin.

The phone had rung at half past four in the morning. I lay in the darkness staring towards the shrilling shape, willing myself to extract an arm from underneath the warm duvet. I resented the disturbance, but the darkness and the timing aroused in me a curious feeling of unease. It was with such misgiving that I picked up the receiver. 'Yes? . . . I mean, hello.'

'Mrs Trench?'

'Yes, that's me.'

'This is Sergeant Rusted, West Hampstead Police Station.' I felt my sleepiness fade away, and a miserable selfconsciousness descend like a cloak over me.

'Yes, Sergeant, what can I do for you at this early hour of the morning?'

'We have one of your boys here. He gave us your telephone number. I wondered if you'd come over and help us clear up this mess he's in.'

'Okay, give me twenty minutes. By the way, which of my lads is it?' I knew I didn't need to ask; it could only be Martin.

'Grieves – Martin Grieves.'

Mrs Grieves had visited the comprehensive school five years ago, when Martin was still at his primary school, because she was worried about him and about the impending transfer to secondary school. He was stealing large sums of money from her; furthermore, he could not read. Mrs Grieves had guilt feelings about him because she felt Martin had had less of her attention than her other two children. So, commendably, she was trying to organise support for him at the local comprehensive before he actually arrived.

Sure enough he needed it when the time came. Immediately he acquired a reputation for stealing among his classmates, and indeed he was virtually a non-reader, and could neither write nor spell. He did not mix well with other children because he was a bully and spiteful. He was enrolled in Spark within six months, and within four weeks had been arrested by the police with another three of our children, breaking and entering a garage at the end of our road. The following week he was excluded from school for attacking and beating up another first-year. All this produced a flurry of activity by the professionals and assessment of Martin's needs became a long-drawn-out affair. This was mostly due to the now not-so-willing-to-help Mrs Grieves, who had got scent of the descending pack of the Establishment who were recommending boarding school for the maladjusted for her child.

Indeed, Mrs Grieves was positively fearful and resistant, and unless carefully nurtured would try to take her son back to Ireland, or transfer him to another school, or simply would have kept him at home, if any precipitate attempt to consign him to a residential place was made. In fact, Mrs Grieves, a small, pale, fragile lady with the furtiveness of a fox, managed to outwit the whole Establishment with stubborn effectiveness by never appearing for meetings or appointments, so the procedure of signing consent forms by parents for special education was admirably foiled and Martin's last four years of education were to remain fundamentally Spark's responsibility.

Now fifteen, a spotty youth covered in blackheads on an expressionless, mask-like face, he sat in the upstairs schoolroom chewing the skin round his bitten-down fingernails, tilting his chair backwards. Lunch was finished and Sammy and Rod were on washing and drying-up duties by the sink while the rest of us sat informally round the central table drinking coffee.

'Yer ain't got one Sal, 'ave yer?' I pretended I had not been listening to their conversation, for often one gleans more information this way than by appearing over-eager to join in.

'Got what?'

'Yer ain't got a video recorder, 'ave yer?'

'No, I haven't, have you?' All eight boys in the room stared at me, as if noticing me for the first time. I smiled. 'Have I said something sensational?' We looked at each other awkwardly. Piers, his eyes slightly hooded, his chalky pallor as white as the scouring powder he was sprinkling over the work surfaces, replied,

'Nah, Sal, it's just we've all got one. Funny that yer ain't, that's all.'

'Why is it funny?'

''Cause yer middle-class an' all that,' Sammy said from the depths of the soap suds.

'What's class got to do with it? The reason I haven't bought a video is because I can't afford it.'

'Bet Chris and Nick would like one,' Martin contributed.

'I'm sure they would. I wouldn't mind one myself.' I paused before adding, 'Have you *all* got one?' They all nodded. It was one of life's paradoxes that these kids might not have enough food in the house for their dinner, nor enough bedding to go round, but they all had a television set and video recorder. I never thought further about this conversation till a few days later when in the early evening the doorbell rang. Martin was standing there, wiping the perspiration from his brow, looking very pleased with himself.

''Ere, I got yer and the kids something.' Without invitation, he picked up a large cardboard box at his feet, brushed past me and went into the drawing-room. I followed and Nick followed me. We stood there with a sense of expectancy as Martin opened the huge box. His spotty face triumphant, he pulled out a shining new video recorder.

'For yer, a hundred nicker,' he pronounced solemnly. He must have seen my look of shock. 'It's okay Sal, all above board, yer see I have this mate who flogs 'em and I told 'im you ain't rich, so he agreed yer could 'ave it cheap like.' I grew uncomfortably stiff with suspicion, while Nick was on his knees beside it almost trembling with excitement. Martin shuffled from one foot to another, still awaiting my rapturous acceptance of this square box before me.

'You mean it's off the back of a lorry,' I said eventually. Martin considered me with distaste and cleared his throat meaningfully.

'Nah, yer got it all wrong. It's clean. Promise yer. Come on, I'll fix it.' He knelt down next to the exuberant Nick and began putting wires into the television.

'It's no good, Martin, we can't test it, we don't possess a tape,' my youngest explained with genuine dismay.

95

'Don't think I didn't think of that.' From his pocket he withdrew a tape and handed it to Nick. I stared at this brand new machine. I stared at the brand-new cardboard box which had the words 'video recorder' stamped all over it.

'Tell me, why is your friend letting me have it for a hundred pounds when it must be worth twice that amount?' I asked suspiciously. Martin was showing Nick the knobs and didn't bother to look up.

'Sal, 'e's a mate. Don't yer 'ave friends who 'elp yer aht? Go on, sit dahn and watch this.' He motioned me towards my own sofa. I felt thrown off balance. I wanted to believe him. Why shouldn't I believe him? After all, if he had nicked it, it wouldn't have come in a marked glossy box, unless of course it was one of a large haul. The explanation he gave was within the bounds of the possible, I argued. Why couldn't I accept his word, why was I being so negative when I should be so delighted at the offer of such a bargain? What a damp squib I was, when this kid had taken such trouble, and look at Nick, his face alight with enthusiasm.

Suddenly, I could find none but the best reasons to overcome my inherent distrust. 'Okay, Martin, we'll have it, but I can't pay you tonight. I don't keep that sort of cash in the house. I'll go to the bank tomorrow morning, and you can have it to give to your friend tomorrow evening.' He looked at the back of his smudged, dirty hands.

'Don't worry, Sal, my mate can wait – no 'urry. T'morrow be fine. I'll see yer then,' and he left us as he arrived, by the front door.

I walked to the police station in the below-freezing temperature, feeling preposterously foolish. How weak and naive I had been in believing Martin's story. I was furious and curiously insulted by his cheating me and placing me in such a compromising situation. I blamed him bitterly, when I should have been blaming myself. Sergeant Rusted was waiting for me and guided me into a small room empty apart from a table and two chairs. He lit a cigarette and inhaled.

'Sorry to call you out at this ungodly hour, but I want to

clear it up before I go off duty. I suppose you know what it's about?'

'I'm not sure – you tell me,' I lied unhappily.

'Mrs Trench, there was a burglary yesterday afternoon, two roads down from where you live. A video was taken and the culprit left his trade mark.'

'Oh!' I said owlishly. 'What's his trademark?'

'Footprints on the garden bed outside the smashed window. Fingerprints on the windowsill.'

'Are they Martin's?'

'Yes – they've been matched, but he hasn't admitted to it. He just said I was to contact you – so tell me what do you know?'

'Have you informed his mother?' I prevaricated.

'Yes, we picked him up at home. So where do you fit into this?' I stared at him in that blind, unseeing way, when anguish and hostility are the only visible echoes of a dented pride.

'I don't fit into this. Unless you want to have me up as the receiver of stolen property. I think the missing video is in my drawing-room,' I muttered miserably and slowly relayed the story of the previous evening. When I had finished he said,

'I'll send a constable back with you.' He paused. 'Would you object if we search the rest of your house?'

'I'm not a bloody fence,' I screamed angrily, and then dropping my voice, 'Yes, of course you can. I've nothing to hide. I would be grateful if you could wait a little – I mean everybody's asleep at the moment. They might get a bit of a shock if you start tramping through the bedrooms. Meanwhile, can I see Martin before I go?'

He lit another cigarette and watched me closely before answering. 'I'm afraid not – we have to get a statement off him first.' This was quite a relief for at that very moment I could have committed first-degree murder in the police cell of West Hampstead police station.

A mournful Martin appeared two days later and thrust a badly spelled note into my hand, apologising for his lies. But what vexed me most was that he knowingly and willingly would have robbed me of a hundred pounds. Four years with us had obviously taught him nothing and when I had shed all my tears of disappointment for the betrayal, the elaborate pretence, I was calm, on a plane of unexpected acceptance. It was the next day that I went and bought a video recorder.

Chapter 11

One of my most disagreeable duties as director of Project Spark was fund-raising. I hated it. Nevertheless, as my trustees were quick to point out, I was the best person to do it for I knew more about Spark than anyone else. Also I was good at it: (a) because I knew my subject inside out and outside in; (b) because of my obsession with Spark, I totally believed every word I uttered and the truth shone through; (c) I was a woman with magnetism. In order to market the idea of Spark, whether it be to an individual or a company, I had to sell myself and always at the end of the day I felt like a prostitute having sold my soul.

There were over 100,000 educational charities registered with the Department of Education and Science. The reasons for these large numbers are perhaps explained in part by the fact that the law, while allowing a wide definition of charities in general, accorded educational charities special status. Among other advantages, they could hold property in perpetuity and they also enjoyed an advantageous tax position. Spark needed approximately £12,000 a year and had minimum overheads, as I ran most of the administration in my spare time. To assist me, on an occasional basis, we employed the most patient and indispensable chartered accountant who also audited our annual accounts.

Initially Spark, not being a large or well-established charity like Oxfam or Save The Children, did not receive regular donations, either under deeds of covenant or from supporters who responded to annual appeals. As I was to discover, a charity's most valuable asset was its list of names and addresses of those who gave to its cause, for a person who had once made a donation was a potential future giver, and could properly be approached from time to time. All donations meant extra work, for they had to be duly recorded and receipted, and if I knew the donor I always insisted that I wrote to thank him or her personally. I had neither the time nor the energy to organise fêtes, dinner-dances or Christmas cards, though one year I did arrange a very successful musical evening with the Yehudi Menuhin School. My main source of fund-raising was writing to the major industries asking for an interview – if I was not rejected by that time, inevitably I came away with a cheque. Also I approached well-known educational trusts who would visit the Project for the morning – again, I was usually confident that if they agreed to visit, they would support us.

Like all of life, sometimes providence played its part. For instance, one evening I was invited to dine with friends in Chelsea. Among the ten guests was Harold Haywood, then the director of the Royal Jubilee Trust. We spent the evening talking and he invited me to submit my latest annual report and what other papers I had on Spark. Within the week I had made an appointment with his secretary to see him. Dressed up for the arctic weather, I took the Underground to Chancery Lane to keep my appointment with Harold Haywood. It was bitterly cold and I arrived with icicles hanging from my ears and nose. Fortunately I was ten minutes early which gave me time to thaw and drip in the exquisitely posh waiting-room. The décor was all in royal blue with photos of the Queen and Prince Charles prominent on the white walls.

I was shown up to Harold's office by a well-groomed secretary. 'Hello, good to see you again,' he said cheerfully, coming across from his desk to shake me warmly by the hand as if we were old friends. Immediately we fell into discussion about the difficulties of raising money for small charities. I was surprised he didn't ask me too many questions about Project Spark, but I had sent the various papers for him to peruse earlier in the week. He appeared fairly optimistic that his Trust could support us and I left laden with application forms and various names and addresses to follow up. On the landing of the first floor he showed me their committee room, furnished by Buckingham Palace, and then remarked how he liked my boots. I had forgotten to change them after walking Dog. I was wearing my Dr Martens!

I was often invited to give talks – to religious groups, to women's movements, to schools and colleges, and even prisons. I rarely rejected these requests, not because I enjoyed them – indeed if the truth be known I dreaded these evenings – but because I felt obliged, accountable, honour-bound to share the beliefs and philosophies of Spark with the public. I was a nervous performer and would often be found in the toilets preceding my talk, throwing up.

There were also many dividends – the audience often made a collection for Spark. Oundle School organised a sponsored swim and raised a thousand pounds. The Yehudi Menuhin School played at Winchester College and the sale of tickets brought in over seven hundred pounds. Sevenoaks School, after I had given the senior forms a talk, offered me two fifth-years annually, after they had finished their O-levels, to help in the Project. I must admit I preferred addressing young people, purely because it appealed to my moral sensibility: here I could encourage the advantaged young to help the disadvantaged young.

There were other bonuses for me personally, such as travelling. I was invited to Australia, to America, to Europe, to expound my own philosophies, my past work with the down-and-outs and my present work with Spark. I have met people all over the world who have given me the most extraordinary hospitality and kindness for which I shall be eternally grateful. In Oslo, I couldn't have been treated better if I had been the Queen of England; in Austria, the Viennese Steiner School opened their hearts to me; in Boston and New York the colleges warmed to my British sense of humour; and so the money for Spark was raised. I may have hated speaking, but we all benefited from it, each and every one in Spark.

The teachers' pay dispute, which had lasted for over a year, and led to thousands of children missing their lessons, had been settled. All the unions were calling off strike action. I was overjoyed. Now we could get back to the job of educating our children. I attended two weekly meetings that morning with a new optimism when the deputy head of the local comprehensive apologised for being late: he had had to organise sending some fourth-years home.

'But the strike is over,' I claimed indignantly.

'Oh yes, the strikes are over, but the NUT is not a party to the latest deal, drawn up by the conciliation service, ACAS, so half the teaching force will continue to disrupt schools by refusing to cover for absent colleagues, to attend parent and staff meetings, and to take part in school activities outside school hours. So when there's no cover, I'm bound to send the kids home.'

My elation and optimism vanished. It was not the peace settlement we had been led to believe.

After one week back at school, following two weeks' strike holiday and a further week for half-term, my Spark children were noticeable for their presence. Thomas was still not allowed to attend his maths lessons for swearing at the teacher – the said lady was now away ill, so I couldn't even sort out a compromise with her. Freddy had been caught the day before in the junior girls' toilets and Riki had wandered in late, looking pale and heavy-eyed, claiming that his mother made the best double tequila this side of Mexico. Looking at him I was quite prepared to believe him. Emily arrived with her hand swathed in bandages and stating the obvious, that there was no point in her attending her typing lessons as her hand was at present unusable. We all took the easy way out and agreed, but gave her no consolation by enquiring how the injury occurred. It was good to have them back, wheeling and dealing, manoeuvring and manipulating, keeping us on our toes, for life was exceptionally dull without them all.

Next morning, I was on a bus when I saw Emily with a group of girls wandering towards school; it was ten past eleven. I decided on my return that it was time to have further words with her mother. There was apparently no way in which school seemed to be able to check her whereabouts once she had registered present first thing in the morning. I supposed that if a teacher did notice she was absent from his lesson he was pleased and had a less disrupted class. Damn the child.

The freeze was over, and spring in the air had gone to Dog's head. No longer aggrieved by the presence of the cats, I found Dog copulating with Rambo, who, looking like a miniature toy against the height and bulk of Dog, wasn't quite sure what was happening.

Meanwhile Thomas, the new Spark boy, was in further trouble. I was phoned by one of his teachers, who unfortunately suffered from obesity. Apparently, in her last lesson he arrived late and instead of settling down to his work, began flicking through some sex magazines and pointing to some beautiful exotic females with next to no clothes on. He demanded attention by asking her in front of the class why she didn't look like them.

'I won't have him back in my lessons,' she hollered down the phone. I commiserated and agreed that his behaviour was quite unacceptable and that he would have to come and do his work here during her periods. When Thomas arrived a few minutes later I noticed that he had not brought the magazines with him, and to add insult to injury was not penitent. In fact, quite the reverse, he was delighted to have been thrown out of her class and no doubt had executed the performance for this very reason. I was awe-struck when I went into school for a meeting directly after this episode. In the staffroom on the noticeboard was a resolution from the junior school council consisting of children between the ages of eleven and thirteen. It read: 'Detentions don't make badly-behaved pupils more obedient, they do destroy teacher/class relationships; the people that cause the detentions don't turn up. Therefore teachers should learn how to control the class and stop putting kids, who are probably innocent, at an inconvenience. We propose an end to class detentions.' Soon there would be no sanctions for the teachers; we were fast approaching William Golding's *Lord of the Flies* situation, when little monsters like the new Spark child would run amok and be given credit marks for humiliating and destroying those adults called teachers.

A Spark teacher came in looking ghastly. Bloodshot eyes

in dark hollows, pallor like the white cliffs of Dover, such that even the Spark kids couldn't fail to notice this skeleton of the human race.

'On heroin, then?' the new boy asked with deep concern. Emily looked up from her work and studied the sick woman before her.

'Nah,' she butted in. 'Look, she's got a sore – she's been glue sniffing, haven't you, miss?'

'Shut up all of you,' I interposed firmly. 'We don't nag you like this when you don't feel well . . .'

'When we don't feel well we don't come in,' someone remarked.

'We don't come in when we do feel well,' another petal chirped up. This time I raised my voice.

'Okay you guys, you've had your fun, now settle down to work.' As I left the room I glanced across at the teacher and mentally bet ten to one she would not be vertical by the end of the morning.

I had arranged a meeting with the head to discuss the growing problem of alcoholism among our teenagers. I was in school standing outside his office, talking to the school secretary when the door opened. As I was about to enter, one of the clerks pushed me aside and showed some parents in. The door was shut.

'Hold it,' I exclaimed to the clerk, 'I have a meeting in there now. What's going on?' She looked apprehensive and apologetically explained that the head had agreed to see some parents. Damn it, if the head hadn't the courtesy to keep appointments, what was this world coming to? I knocked on the door without waiting for an answer, and went in. The head jumped up from his chair.

'I'm so sorry, Sally, I can't see you at the moment, can you wait?' I muttered that I could not, and slammed the door shut and went home to cook the evening meal, seething with indignation. Mohammed came to the mountain, for half an hour later the head was on the doorstep apologising, so I gave him a cup of coffee and we sat down in the drawing-room to discuss our business. Meanwhile, the Spark teacher was giving a spelling test to the Spark kids, taking words from a spelling book for eleven-year-olds, our children being fourteen and fifteen. Our scholar was Riki, with the high mark of nineteen out of forty. The new Spark boy had only nine right. I believed that this incredibly low standard was nothing to do with their deprivation or their problems, but the extraordinary belief of recent thinking in education that children should not have to learn parrot-fashion.

'Right,' I said to the teacher, 'back to the basics. You'll have to give them a spelling test every week and the winner will get a Mars bar. At the end of term, the child who can spell correctly three-quarters of that spelling book I will personally take to the pub.'

Alcoholism had not been a great problem in Spark, partly because they spent their lunch hour with us, when other kids were able to slip down to the pub from school, and partly because, officially, we had them occupied, either here or in school, for the full day's timetable. Of course, their evenings were not in our control, and it was becoming obvious to those dealing with adolescents that under-age drinking was becoming a grave problem.

Since the sixties there has been a widespread belief that the problem of adolescent delinquency, whether it be drinking, glue sniffing or taking drugs, is a purely modern phenomenon. In fact, adolescent delinquency is as old as adolescence itself. The nineteenth century saw a rash of adolescent gangs terrorising the cities, not only for money but for purely delinquent reasons as well. For example, the word 'hooligan' harks back to the Hooley gang, a group of young teenagers who used to terrorise South London in the last century. Perhaps delinquency was not such a widespread problem in those days, because children were sent out to work at a much earlier age, and this prevented the majority from having the time (for free time is a very important variable) to commit delinquent acts. Also, children of those times faced much harsher penalties than children of today. If a teenager were to steal a car today he might find himself on probation, but if a teenager of the last century were to steal a horse, he could very likely find himself hung or deported.

It is absolutely natural for adolescents to go through a rebellious stage. They find themselves between childhood and adulthood and yet feel treated as neither. They want the terms of adulthood, but they still seek the support, emotional, physical and financial, of childhood. They tend to rebel against every form of authority whether it be parental, official or just other members of society and tend to commit acts which show their disdain for authority. They feel they cannot associate with either adults or younger children for neither group 'understands' them, so they form into tightly-knit peer groups such as skinheads, mods, rockers, punks, goths and casuals. With youth clubs being closed down, teenagers no longer have anywhere to go except the pubs, where there is an obligation to drink. Boredom, not alcohol, I believe is one of the main factors in juvenile delinquency.

With increasingly more time on their hands than previously and increasingly less motivation to occupy themselves, more and more bored juveniles turn to drink. It is not helpful that drinking is socially acceptable and that alcohol is freely available. Pubs are not particularly strict whom they serve, nor are off-licences, corner shops and some supermarkets, where they buy. The risks to shopkeepers, publicans and to the teenagers themselves are minimised as the law is rarely enforced. Certainly, I do not believe that changing the licensing laws to the system which prevails in most of the world, of free hours, is going to alleviate the problem as so many experts have declared. Just look at France and Italy with much higher levels of deaths due to alcohol (ten times higher) than the UK.

Another reason for the increase in alcohol consumption by the young must be due partly to the increased amounts of money teenagers have for their own personal use. Figures of between fifteen and twenty pounds a week are not uncommon, and especially in the case where parents are divorced, the money is handed out as a substitute for parental love. On balance I found the old Spark kids preferred to spend their money on things like music and music equipment, cigarettes and clothes. But there was a new breed of Spark children being sent to me, whose main purpose in life seemed to be to get as drunk as possible as quickly as possible, and this was the reason I decided to take them to the pub once in a blue moon, on special occasions, to educate them about controlled drinking.

Chapter 12

Our Spark new boy, Thomas, was causing problems. In school he disrupted, stole and truanted. In the first four weeks of his fourth year, three option changes had been made in a vain attempt to put together a timetable offering some hope, but it had become clear that he could not follow a full timetable. They thought he could cope with English, maths, science, games and art if there was constant support and supervision, and this was when Spark was called in. I did not express my doubts about the lad to the teacher, but asked her to run some tests. They revealed that Thomas was very bright. His attainment was not exceptional, but his potential was, and for him to be languishing in low-level fourth-year sets would be valid only if by doing so his considerable psychological problems were being soothed. In fact they were almost certainly being exacerbated.

Here was a common conundrum with our brighter children. If they were sent back into school full-time to follow full timetables, attractive as this was in terms of stretching them by moving them into higher sets and thus attempting to earn them favourable (O-level) recommendations, they would behave so badly that the class teacher would be forced to exclude them, or they would just collapse under the pressure and not appear. It was a delicate balance we sought and often as not failed to find. Thomas was a bully and a fighter, and put his mouth where his fist was all too frequently. He started fights and finished them on his feet, gloating. Kids were scared of him, scared enough to flock round him. With his height and long arms, he appeared to tower over them. He knew he was a smart cat and he knew that I knew he was just a little crazy. But I was not prepared for the outcome.

I was in school when it was reported to me that he had led a gang of kids, while on a school trip to the Science Museum, on to the Underground without tickets, leaving the teacher behind queuing at the ticket office. When I got home I went up to the schoolroom and asked him to come and see me when his lesson had finished. He kicked the drawing-room door open.

'Come in, Thomas, close the door will you?' He kicked it shut.

'What yer want?'

'To talk to you.'

'Wot abaht?'

'Yesterday.' He smiled a twisted smile.

'Oh yeah, so . . . ?'

'I hear you jumped a train with some other kids without a ticket.'

'Wot's the big deal?' His eyes were roaming round the room.

'There's no big deal, Thomas; it's just you've now been banned from school outings and I want to know whether it's justified,' I calmly replied. For the first time he looked directly at me.

'Justified?' He spat the word.

'Yes, do you know what that word means?' He glared at me.

'Yeah.'

'It comes from the word justice.' He twiddled his fingers.

'Yeah, I knah, so what?'

'Well, I don't like the idea of my kids in Spark being blacklisted if it's not deserved, so I thought I'd ask you whether it was justified.'

'Yes, s'pose so.'

'So you do admit that you were in the wrong?' I asked casually. He sat up straight, uncrossing his legs.

'Nah, I ain't said that.'

'Now Thomas, you're a very intelligent young man, so stop pretending you're thick. We both know you never said that.' He was becoming impatient and somewhat frustrated with my indirect methods of attack.

'Hell, Sal, wot do yer want me to say?'

'Good heavens! It's nothing to do with what I want you to say. What do you want to say? I only wanted to make sure you were not being picked on as the leader of the gang,' I said slyly. He thought about this for a second, realising the implications, for he did not want to deny that he was the leader, the hero of the day.

'I weren't picked upon,' he replied sullenly.

'So you were the leader of this unruly gang that barged and pushed on to the train knocking people right, left and centre?'

'No one picks on me,' he threw his head back and curled his lower lip.

'Well, that's fine. Then it's all true and you're guilty,' I pointed out. He knew he was trapped. He flashed his eyes at me and then suddenly laughed.

'So wot yer goin' to do abaht it?'

I rose from my chair and walked across to the french windows. He fidgeted uncomfortably.

'Well, Sal?' His voice had lost the bullying tone.

'Hmm.' I turned round. 'Sorry, what?' I appeared absent-minded.

'Well, wot yer going to do to punish me?'

'Ah, you think I should punish you, then?' I asked innocently. He pulled at his ear and made a clicking sound with his tongue on the roof of his mouth as I walked back to my chair.

He swore at me quietly, slowly and deliberately. I did not respond. I had won every round so far, and I was not about to lose my cool now. He wanted a direct confrontation; this was his way to fight.

'You were asking how I was going to punish you?' He sat tight-lipped, as if willing himself not to open his mouth to fall further into the tangled web I was weaving round him.

'Well, it would be a bit repetitive to ban you from Spark

outings as School has done, wouldn't it?' He was clenching his fists, his knuckles were white. 'So I think the only answer is the bathroom.'

'The bathroom?'

'Yes, we'll put a desk up in the bathroom and you can work there.'

'Wot's wrong with the schoolroom?'

'Ah! Well, you see, you admitted that you had not acted in a civilised way, so I don't think you should mix with the rest of Spark until you can behave properly.'

He looked at me incredulously.

'Yer ain't 'aving me on, are yer?'

'Indeed not, my doubting Thomas: this is straight down the line. I want you to go and work on your own in the bathroom for the next week.'

'Wot about lunch then?'

'We'll bring you your lunch,' I replied cheerfully.

'Wot if I get stuck on the work?'

'You can call the teacher, you're only two rooms away from the schoolroom and you can have the door open.'

'I don't f—— believe this.'

'You will, my dear boy, you will,' I said affably. 'Come on, let's go and see if the desk fits.'

'I'm not f—— putting a desk in the f—— bathroom,' he declared.

'I didn't ask you to, did I? Come on.' I was wondering what my next move would be if he didn't follow, but I need not have worried for he came after me up the stairs and stood and watched me heave a folded desk into the bathroom.

'Wot if they want to use the bathroom?'

'They can use the one downstairs.'

'I ain't sitting in there,' he said defiantly as I carried a chair in.

'Why not? What's wrong with it? It's on the small side, I agree, but it's bright and clean. I only painted it three months ago.'

'I don't care about the decorations, do I? I don't want to be on my own. I want to be in the schoolroom wiv the others.'

'Thomas, you're not scared of being on your own?' I exclaimed.

110

'Yer twist everything I say. I don't mind being on my own.'

'Great! Then you won't mind being in here will you?' He gave me an angry glance and walked out into the corridor. I looked at my watch. School had ended twenty minutes ago.

'Can I go now?'

'Surely, I'll see you tomorrow Thomas.'

'Like hell you will,' he shouted behind him as he descended the stairs.

It was a gamble, but I reckoned the cards were better than evens, for his ego was gluttonous for adoration and attention and he would have neither if he stopped coming to Spark, where he felt captain of the ship. It was important to him what the other children thought of him and that was the first sign to me that he did care.

The following morning he skulked in and without a show of defiance, he took himself into the bathroom where he spent the rest of the week. From that day on, the bathroom was known as 'the cell' and a folded-up desk was kept in there permanently beside the sink. Its very presence became a deterrent and often I heard my teacher say to a pupil, 'You don't want to go to the bathroom do you?' I wondered what a stranger would make of it, on hearing such a threat.

Slowly, we tamed Thomas to our ways, but within three months he was in court on five charges of theft and on this occasion I did not attend, nor offer to be a character witness. The problem, I had thought, with Thomas, was that he was amoral. He enjoyed destruction and did not appear to care. I was wrong, he did care, but time was against us in Spark, for he needed more skills and professional help than we could provide. He reminded me of the H-Bomb: it had the potential to destroy us all, but harnessed, it could provide an endless source of useful power.

Thomas reminded me of a similar lad, called Dick, who also had an incredible gap between potential and performance. When tested, his IQ level was 130 but his spelling age was eight and a half. The difference may have been explicable in terms of the compulsion he had to show off. Sometimes he would express himself in class discussion

111

reasonably well and then, for no apparent reason, he would launch into shouted nonsense. Often he banged and slammed around the schoolroom simply to announce his presence, but if his histrionics failed to distract our Spark-hardened tutor group, his disruptions assumed a desperate quality. He would cut his T-shirt in several places with a razor blade and then pin the severed ends together in such a way that the pins drew his own blood. Then he sat there with the blood dripping down the pin and over his fingers. Another time, Dick was frantically demanding her attention and the teacher refused to stop what she was doing. He rose from his chair and crossed the room. With all eyes fastened on him, without flinching, he pierced the pin through his nose.

One evening, late, I had had a bath and was preparing to go to bed when I heard a noise outside the French windows. I disregarded it, assuming it was the cats, but then I heard a definite tapping on the glass. I threw back the curtains and peered into the dark. It was Dick. I opened the window. 'What the hell are you up to?' I demanded. 'It's after midnight.' He leapt into the room. His cheeks were suffused with crimson, and his feverish, possessed eyes shone with a hectic brilliance. He was breathing hard and his skin was clammy. Involuntarily, I waved to him to sit down. I knew the smell of trouble. I waited for him to speak. He took his time, slowly undoing the buttons to his jacket first. 'Well, I'd like to know what's going on?' I finally said. He had taken his jacket off and was now stripping off his sweater and I could see the damp patches of his T-shirt where he had perspired heavily. My waiting policy had little effect and certainly was not therapeutic for me. I was tired, irritable and impatient.

'For goodness sake, Dick, what are you doing here?' As soon as I said these words, I realised my compromising situation. Here we both were in my bedroom in the middle of the night, me in my nightdress and him in a T-shirt and jeans. Ever since he had arrived in Spark, he had quite clearly been craving for some expression of love: the noisy showing-off, the irritating aberrations of behaviour, the boisterous vivacity all were clear signs. Over the months I had shown him a new set of values, I had shared his doubts as well as his certainties, I had offered sincerity, conviction and enthusiasm and I had won his affection and trust. Oh Lord! Had he created a deliberate situation here to test my love? I was deciding upon unobtrusive vigilance when the doorbell rang. Dick shivered which gave me my first chance.

'Put your sweater on, you'll get cold. There's no heating on at this time of the morning.'

'Don't answer it, Sal.' He was not shivering, he was shaking.

'Why? Who do you think it is?' It rang again.

'How should I know?' he replied too snappily.

'Well, there's only one way of finding out.' I leapt to my feet and, before the whole household awoke, I opened the front door. Two police officers stood in the shadow of the porch.

'Good evening, madam, we're sorry to disturb you, but we saw a young man turn into your drive and we saw your light on and wondered if we could search your garden?'

'No need for that, he's in the drawing-room. Come in.'

'Thank you, madam.' I refrained from asking what he had done. For all they knew he could have lived here. I followed them into the drawing-room-cum-bedroom. The French windows were wide open and Dick had vanished. I must admit I felt some relief, for this situation was so much easier to deal with than adolescent sex.

'Ah! He's gone.' I was about to close the windows.

'Wait a minute, madam, can we just look out there?'

'Be my guest.' The two of them disappeared into the blackness and I went into the kitchen to make coffee, having given up any thought of sleep. They returned some time later, obviously having scoured the neighbourhood.

'May we ask you a few questions?'

'Certainly.'

'What is the boy's name?'

'Dick Lindsay.'

'Is he related to you?'

'No.'

'So, madam, what was he doing here in your drawing-room?' I wanted to giggle and tell them what my fears had been, and how delighted I was that they had arrived. Instead I replied,

'I think he must have known you were after him and he came here either to hide or for protection.'

'Why here, madam?'

'Well, he comes to school here, it's like a second home to him.'

'So where does he live?'

'I'll have to look it up.' I went to my desk and found the book and told them.

'Thank you, madam, for your help.' He closed his notebook and finished his coffee.

'Hold it! My turn to ask questions. What's he meant to have done?' The officer coughed mildly, as if out of courtesy.

'He was seen in Medway Road at eleven thirty putting newspaper through the letterbox of number twenty-three and setting fire to it.' We both stared at each other in shock. Number twenty-three Medway Road was Dick's home.

'Oh Lordy, Lord. Poor Dick. What are you going to do?' The constables stood up to leave.

'Our colleague is at the house now interviewing the owners, at least, the parents – we'll find the boy.'

I took the mugs into the kitchen to wash them up, thinking about Dick. Adolescence is such a difficult time for children. Love for parents tends to decline at that age as they clash with their authority and realise their fallibility. Their feeling that 'they don't understand' may amount to a fierce, and often secret, resentment against one or both parents.

'Have they gone?' The voice so startled me from my thoughts that I jumped. I swung round to see Dick standing there, nervously twitching.

'Where have you come from?'

'The larder.'

'You wretch! You mean you were here all the time they were searching for you in the garden.' He grinned.

'I opened the French windows to get them off my scent – clever, don't you think?'

'Well, I think you'd better sit down and tell me all about it, don't you?' His eyes looked reproachfully at me. 'I know you tried to set fire to your home, what I don't comprehend is why you did it from outside the house.'

'They'd locked me out.'

'And you hadn't a key?'

'No, they took my key off me months ago. Said I weren't responsible enough.'

'They both work, don't they.'

'Yeah.'

'So, how were you meant to get in after school?'

'I weren't. That was the point. They didn't want me in the house on my own. They don't trust me.'

'So when you left here in the afternoons, what did you do?'

'Walked the streets, went down to play on the fruit machines.'

'When do they come home?'

'About seven, sometimes later.'

'What did they expect you to do?' He shrugged his shoulders and looked away.

'They don't care, they never have.'

'Of course they do, Dick, they just don't know how to express it, probably.' His eyes flashed at me and he thumped the table.

'Don't you tell me about my bloody parents, you don't know them.'

'I'm sorry, Dick, you're quite right. I have no right to make any judgments.'

— 'I don't know why I was born. They never wanted me, they've never taken any interest in me, they never wanted me around. In three months, you've shown more interest in me than they've shown in fourteen years.' His anger and anguish, like love and hate, were twins. Tears were pouring down his face. 'They don't love me, but they won't let me go. They have to possess me, have power over me to make themselves feel important. Because they have nothing, they have to make themselves something and I'm the victim for their sense of power. I'd be better off dead than this.'

My heart went out to this boy. I did not have to pretend that I understood, for I had had the very same thoughts in my childhood. He was expressing those passions of absurd

115

misery, of bitterness, of frustration that recurred like a violent nightmare, where one has been hurled repeatedly again and again through the dark obsessive afflictions of one's parents and left exhausted and battered. Each time to rise again, however bruised and scarred, full of absurd hope and good resolutions, only to repeat the hurling and battering for further confirmation that they will not forgive human frailty. Eventually there is no shaft of tempered sunlight, for hope withers over many years and is finally devoured by the unfurling creeper of cruelty – the progressive destruction of human dignity.

Drained of anger and anguish, with no tears left, Dick sat there in a dim, exhausted dream. I sat opposite, the solid comfortable woman, full of common sense and understanding. I realised with some shame that though I was an adult in his presence, I had remained a child with these same thoughts. I put out my hand and he grasped it. It was sufficient contact to break his solitude – and my shame.

'Sorry,' he muttered.

'No need to be – you don't need to feel guilt or shame with me. But, my dear, listen to me, for I think you've helped me.' His wet, clouded eyes looked up.

'Helped you?'

'Yes, I had not realised that I'm still suffering, too. I often wondered why I had chosen this path. I'm no saint, so why am I doing this work?'

''Cause you care about us.'

'Sure I do, but what motivated me at sixteen to go and look after the dirty old meths drinkers on the bomb sites?'

'I dunno. I thought it was Christianity.'

'If only I had been that worthy. No, it was because I wanted to be needed.'

'Sal, it's turned out all right for you, hasn't it?'

'Yes, I suppose it has. Spark has compensated for my hopeless love and become a kind of obsession that's driven me on; kept me busy; kept me doing, so I don't have to face my own pain.' He puckered his eyebrows.

'What's your pain, Sal?'

'The same as yours, Dick – craving the birthright to be loved.' If an earthquake or a thunderbolt from the sky had blasted down upon us, it would have had no audience at that moment, for we were sharing an unspoken secret of our lifetime. It was as if I had lanced a boil. Suddenly, a peace and stillness descended upon me, as if the elements were obeying a sacred law of calm and silence.

'What chance have I got?' Dick broke the silence.

'Every chance in the world. Just as I had.'

'You believe in me still?' I looked across at the dishevelled image.

'Oh yes, Dick, as long as you don't holler for vengeance.'

He fell asleep in Christopher's room and I experienced a kind of agreeable giddiness, as if I had been born again, and went and lay on my bed to await the dawn. I felt as if I had drunk some old sweet wine, for my mind glided through space, released from the burden that I had subconsciously carried all my life.

Chapter 13

It all began when Bill, aged fourteen, was taken to court for school non-attendance. The family was well known to the social services and educational welfare departments. I had been asked to attend a review meeting on Bill, with the possibility that he would attend our unit as a last desperate measure of social and educational support for this deeply unhappy boy. Nobody was optimistic that we could help him for his emotional and physical deprivation were so deep rooted. But as far as we were concerned, this was just another kid in need, consequently another challenge for Spark.

He suffered from severe obesity and lacked even the basic rudiments of hygiene, for which he was constantly teased by his peer group. I met him for a preliminary interview alone, his parents unable or unwilling to attend. He seemed keen to start and we agreed he would follow maths, English, history and cooking courses. In the next month we saw him twice, when he wandered in for lunch. As his mother was not on the phone I wrote to her about her son's absences. I received no reply. I visited the home on many occasions, but either she wasn't in or she refused to open the door. On the third occasion I saw Bill. I sat him down for a serious tête-à-tête.

'If you continue like this you'll find yourself back in court,' I pointed out.

'I know.'

'Don't you mind?'

'Nope.' I tried a different tactic.

'The trouble is Bill, you're putting a noose round your own neck. Because you haven't been to school for years you're really behind now, which is such a shame as you're an intelligent lad and could do well.'

We had managed to keep him long enough to test him on one of the occasions he presented himself at lunchtime. We discovered he had a good grasp of fundamental arithmetic principles at a top junior level, which suggested that his exceptionally poor attendance throughout his secondary schooling was largely responsible for his lack of progress beyond this point. His reading age was that of a twelve-year-old, and judging by his performance on the SRA reading laboratory, we assumed that his comprehension was somewhat lower. As with his maths, we anticipated that his ability to learn may have been impaired by his long period of absence from any kind of education.

I have always made it a custom each day to greet my pupils as they trundle through my kitchen door, by looking into their faces. From the brightness in their eyes or from the slight slant or twist of the mouth, I can usually tell if a child was full of anger or grief. If this was the case, he could come in here as taut as a violin string and any careless word or touch could cause further pain. Every child reacts differently – some find relief when offered sympathy, whereas such kindness can sometimes emphasise pain or even can be taken as interference by others. I had to be able to apprehend and respond to what was going on in the innermost depths of their hearts. The ability to understand, sense and respond to their needs was also the very heart of Spark. Often Bill managed to leave me distinctly ashamed and in grave doubt of these skills.

Another month was to pass before I decided to take action. It was a wet, significantly uniform grey morning when I hammered on Bill's front door. It was not yet eight o'clock and dawn was looking like dusk. To my great surprise the door was opened and in the dark embrace of its archway stood a woman wrapped in what I thought was a blanket, with curves of pink, flabby flesh protruding like

120

slabs of rolled sausages. We stared aghast at one another. She found her voice first. 'Wot yer want?' she slurred, and I caught the first blast of her alcoholic breath. 'Yer from the Council?'

I pushed my way in, saying, 'No, I'm not from the Council. Do you mind if I come in, it's very wet and you'll catch a cold standing there.' I was in the dingy hall before she had time to resist. With the front door closed, the full force of the smell of alcohol and the feeling of pallid damp and staleness hit me. I could see she was outraged by my forceful tactics, but she was drunk and could not find the words to express herself.

'I'm an educational welfare officer,' I began in my awful, pompous way, and then I saw the fungi growing up through the floorboards in the corner. I quickly averted my eyes to another doorway, when I just had to stop in mid sentence. The dim, dawn light was casting rays of dust across the furnitureless room, lighting up, as if in a spotlight, a naked male figure surrounded by empty bottles, prostrate on his back with an erection. In the cold and the sudden quietness I could not formulate my words. I was frozen up. For minutes we stood staring at one another, unresolved. I could see her face quite plainly now, her cheeks puffed by drink, her hair falling like dried pasta over her wrinkled forehead, her blotched lipstick extending her small mouth almost to her ears. She looked the coldest and most hopeless creature imaginable. I braced myself, not daring to look elsewhere but at this dreadful image before me.

'I've come for Bill,' I stuttered in a quiet, drowned voice through the dingy air, pursuing the purpose of my agonising course of duty, 'to take him to school. He hasn't attended school for months, you know.' She continued to stand there wordlessly, clutching like a cat at what I now saw was a curtain. 'Okay if I get him?' I persevered.

She shrugged her shoulders and, turning towards the doorway, she muttered, 'F—— off,' and shambled unsteadily towards the horizontal body on the floorboards. Trembling a little, I ascended the staircase, and as I hesitated at the top step my courage quietly died. Then I heard a snore and a new confused sense of boldness possessed me to shout out loud,

121

'Bill? Bill are you there?' The snoring turned to snorting and a bed creaked as a body turned its weight.

'Bill, it's Sally from Spark. I've come to take you back there.' I began to thump on the door, from behind which came the noises.

'Wot is it?' a voice shouted gruffly.

I repeated myself, 'Bill, it's Sally from Spark.'

'Oh shit!' I heard him groan, and then, 'Don't come in – I'll be down in a minute.'

That day became the first full day Bill attended Spark, and it was to be the first report I was to write to the social services on his home conditions, which was to lead to another court attendance. As a result, Bill was moved to a residential assessment centre. Prior to his presence in court Bill attended school on five days out of a possible thirty-eight. Since he was moved to the assessment centre he never missed a day at Spark. We were so convinced that if he returned to his unsatisfactory home situation Bill would return to his old ways, and so on our recommendation he was moved finally into a children's home. He continued with us and a year later won the prize for the best attendance of the year with a record of ninety-eight per cent. In his final year with us we helped him with his self-imposed diet and he managed to run two and a half miles to raise money for the spina bifida charity. He passed his exams and became our first pupil to go into sixth form and on to college, where he took a community care course. Spark's work was concluded.

Another term had passed and I spent the first day of the holidays filing. Masahide and Christopher returned from their boarding schools and Nick had broken up a week previously. I had just completed the children's reports that were sent out to the teachers in school. It was a tedious task when one was so weary at the end of term, but constructive for those in school. I missed Sue and Gloria, who used to help me write a synopsis of our twenty-two children. The following are examples of reports written by Gloria on six of her fourth-years in Spark Two.

Debby Roe

4th Year   Attendance 96%   Enrolled: April 1986
School subjects: English, Maths, Science, Computer Studies

Debby was sent to us because of persistent truanting and as she was considered quite an intelligent child something had to be done.

Her background is very complicated. Her parents divorced when she was three and she and her brothers lived with their mother until Debby was 7, when it was said that her mother was neglecting the children, but in what sphere it was never mentioned. She then went to live with her father and stepmother in Bristol. School reports from two schools show that Debby was under-achieving and causing great problems. The whole family attended a family guidance clinic but this failed to produce any positive results. A baby was born and due to factors unknown it was decided that Debby and her brothers would go back to their mother. Debby was 14. She started at school and immediately began truanting. Debby's opinion of her time in Bristol differs greatly from the reports. She feels that she was settled and worked well, also that she was happy. We met her mother and she came across as an intelligent and articulate person. However we have since found that she is very unreliable and cannot hold down a job. She also seems unreasonable in some aspects and much more interested in her own affairs and advancement of such and her children take a very definite second place.

Debby is articulate and fairly intelligent, but not as clever as she thinks she is. She uses this to try and outwit us and in other cases she is extremely stupid, bunking when she knows full well that we will find out. The message in this is apparent but often difficult to follow up. She shows her unhappiness in her attitude and temper; mostly to do with situations at home. We have tried to make relations with her mother easier, and Sally has involved her in a few of her family outings, after which she is happy for a short time. She is also very arrogant, unable to take criticism, but able to criticise everyone else. Physically she is tall, thin and has the usual adolescent problems. However she does have gaping teeth and takes a great deal of teasing for this, but manages to handle it quite well. She considers herself better than the others, but in a 'normal' fifteen-year-old environment she wouldn't shine greatly.

She has been referred to the Educational Psychologist.

123

John Fletcher

4th Year   Attendance: 85%   Enrolled: September 1985
School subjects: English, Maths, Drama, Craft and Design

John's behaviour in the classroom was disruptive; loud; unable to sit still; and attention-seeking. He also spent a great deal of his own time with his mother and that was felt not to be 'healthy' for a boy of his age.

On joining Spark he came in for a great deal of teasing due to nasal problems, which made him an excessively noisy and messy eater. This was rectified by informing his mother of the situation and he had a spell in hospital which, although not completely curing the problem, certainly helped. However, the teasing still goes on in a much milder form. He is unpopular with the others both in and out of school, and he doesn't appear to have one particular friend. He didn't come on the Spark holiday and that ostracised him even further, but he doesn't want to be a part of Spark. Outwardly he tries to be 'big' but inwardly he is still very much 'mummy's little boy'. In school his behaviour is slightly improved but not radically and he causes no great problems in Spark. His greatest defence is attack and I don't feel that Spark has done John a great deal of good, although he is happier in himself and more confident, especially after his operation.

Harry Wyatt

4th Year   Attendance: 90%   Enrolled: 1985
School subjects: Maths, English, Craft and Design, Art

Harry comes from a home that is apparently immaculate. Other than that he doesn't talk very much about home.

He was referred to Spark as the school felt that they were 'losing' him. He wouldn't do any work and was playing truant fairly often. He also argued a great deal. He is a large boy for his age, not fat but he is very conscious of his size, and it is what he is teased about most. He is an exceedingly lazy boy who refuses to make any effort and tends to galumph about. However, since coming to Spark there has been a definite improvement. As far as truanting goes, he still does it, but not to such a degree and he is beginning to think twice about that! His whole attitude towards work and play is much more positive and he responds well to praise and competition. In Craft and Design he was doing no work at all, but we did a lot of work at Spark and now he feels that he can handle CD and there has been a great improvement in his

124

attitude within the classroom. Also he is doing a lot more work even down to reading a book. A rude one admittedly!

With the other boys he is popular, and has settled in more easily than anyone else. He rarely loses his temper and even then checks it himself. He also is the one boy who stands up to Chuck and will not be influenced by group activity. He is *very* money orientated and finds it difficult to conceive doing anything which doesn't have any monetary reward.

Because of his maturity and love of money I think we could lose him in the 5th year.

Terry Wells

4th Year   Attendance: 92% Enrolled: September 1986
School subjects: English, Craft and Design, History, Science, Maths

---

Terry is left very much to his own devices at home; his mother doesn't care and his elder brother hasn't really got the time. Father is never mentioned. He spends much of his time at the Sherbutt Youth Club which helps to keep him out of major trouble. He has more self pride than any of the other boys and he does care what others think of him, especially those teachers he likes and respects. Once he has achieved a little it boosts him to work harder; however the reverse applies if he doesn't respect anyone.

When he is angry, frustrated or he feels unfairly treated he argues quite vehemently, but settles down fairly quickly and in most circumstances he doesn't bear a grudge. He is fairly loud and he has a good sense of humour, but hasn't quite learnt limitations and this is where most trouble occurs in Spark – he goes 'over the top', but it is easily settled and he soon bounces back. He is a very popular boy both with his peers and teachers. He has an endearing personality. Outside of school he doesn't mix with other Spark boys, which is probably a very good thing as he can be quite easily influenced.

Terry is one of the most motivated boys we have and he is always willing to 'have a go' and enjoy it. He relates much better to women. He loves Spark and it is a very important part of Terry's life.

Chuck Griffins

4th Year   Attendance: 87%   Enrolled: One term so far!
School subjects: English, Maths, Science, Craft and Design

Where do I begin?! Chuck's background is fairly settled. His father has been unemployed for two years and his mum works

125

as a cook. His two older brothers have been, or are, in prison.

He was, and still can be, a very disruptive pupil to say the least! He was referred to Spark because teachers refused to have him in the classroom. When he came it was him *v.* us, and what a fight. Every day he would argue and push us to the limit, and as he is very good with words this was a great problem. But we persevered and refused to reject him, which was his aim. All the rows culminated in a glorious row which resulted in a confrontation between Sally and Chuck. Happily Sally won and since then he has not been such a problem. He will never be an angel, but relatively he is 100% better.

He still has the loudest mouth and is definitely the 'leader' of the group and influences every boy in one way or another. He is also very involved with the 'goings-on' in the Sherbutt Road Estate which involves criminal activities and he now has about three offences to his name. As he spends so much time in Spark he inevitably gets fed up and does truant to some small degree. I feel that we will lose Chuck after the summer, as his main aim in life is money. He doesn't think in certain situations and tends to act impetuously.

Chuck is to return to O-level Maths after coming second overall in the exams. He is a very intelligent boy, but uses this in the wrong ways.

Dennis Sayle

4th Year   Attendance: 97%   Enrolled: 1986
School subjects: Maths, Art, Life Studies, English

Dennis's background is not very clear – he is the youngest of three children. His father apparently is very strict and his mother very weak. We were asked not to inform the father about Spark as they thought there would be repercussions. However his father found out about Dennis's behaviour and was mentally very cruel to him.

He was referred to Ed. Psych., but that didn't carry on after Dennis came to Spark.

In school he was very aggressive, using both physical and verbal violence; arguing about anything and everything. He also boasted about smoking, glue-sniffing, thieving, etc., to try and sound 'big'. He did steal anything and then tried to sell it back to the owner!

When he came he was not a pleasant boy in either looks or manner and very defensive. He slouched, never smiled, and argued; never listening to any kind of reason and always maintaining that he 'didn't care'. However, after quite a short period he realised that no one was impressed by his antics and that his silly arguing was exactly that – silly, and the other boys told him in no uncertain terms. This then led to him being more relaxed and straightening up, smiling and developing quite a good sense of humour. He forgot to argue and started telling the truth as before he was a compulsive liar. He firstly developed a relationship with Sally through walking the dog and this trust gradually extended.

In school however Dennis is still very difficult to control, he is still silly and argumentative, being involved in a few incidents, but I do feel that gradually he will settle. He has a definite co-ordination problem and does do very stupid things, very immature, thinking in the way that a seven-year-old may think, which is very lateral as opposed to rational. He enjoys cooking, gardening and cycling, all of which require no writing or real thinking, but if I disguise the work he is more able than he has been given credit for. He reads very well and the only real problem is a lack of general knowledge and an inability to write legibly.

Dennis looks on Spark as his second home. He doesn't steal from us, is happy and although immature, developing more confidence daily. Despite school problems I feel that Spark is the best thing that ever happened to Dennis.

Chapter 14

The blossom had beaten the winter and the sun brought new energy and new hope. The summer term was always the easiest for us, but not for the children who sat their final exams like Piers, Freddy and Emily.

Meanwhile, a new term meant new faces and the first was Wonderboy. We first heard of him at a meeting, when his psychiatric social worker and the senior educational psychologist put forth a case that he needed special care or he would flounder. He had attended seven primary schools because of moves of the family home. He lived with his mother, a lone parent, who worked as a gardener. He found it hard to relate to his peer group and was described as an isolated and unhappy child, often in tears and a natural victim. At the age of eleven his mother finally agreed to sign the papers for Wonderboy to attend special boarding school, where he did well and made good use of his psychotherapy sessions. At the age of thirteen and a half years he was subject to a mandatory re-assessment and it was agreed that he should transfer to an ordinary day school.

He had arrived at school a small, rather frail-looking, disorganised boy, who frequently appeared looking grubby and unkempt. He had made no real friends and usually sat on his own with his head in a book. The feeling of the staff was that since his arrival he had done no harm, but they seriously wondered if they were doing him any good.

The school's educational welfare officer first met his

mother in the hospital's casualty department after an incident in school when Wonderboy's nose was broken. The mother then expressed appreciation of what was being done for her son and was friendly and relaxed. However, when she visited the home a week or so later, the circumstances were very different and difficult. Obvious tension was displayed between Wonderboy and his mother and deeply hurtful things were said by both. Subsequent unsuccessful telephone calls to the house revealed that Wonderboy was frequently being left alone in the evenings. On one of her visits, the EWO mentioned the school's concern at his dirty appearance; Mother blamed it on the boy's newspaper round (the print made his hands black) and on the problem of transport which involved his rushing to school. What also became clear on that visit was that the family was suffering severe financial hardship. It was at this point Spark was called in to help on what was described as a temporary basis in order for me to assess him and produce further recommendations.

The first day he presented himself my teacher and I were engrossed in a conversation about one of our lads, when he sarcastically interrupted 'Is there anybody here who's going to bother to teach me?' We both looked at this small, grubby, pompous child standing at the bottom of my staircase and my teacher, recovering quicker than I, guiltily leapt up the stairs to the classroom as grubby, pompous boy followed slowly and condescendingly after her.

During the morning it came to pass that he began to chat. No, this boy was incapable of chatting; sentences were long, affected, starting slowly and building up to a crescendo of speed and noise. He was informing us of his family, and the supply teacher asked him where his grandparents lived. 'Ah!' he sighed like an aged don, 'You will have to forgive me using the word,' short pause followed by the pursing of the lip and the curling of the tongue, like the roll of the drums – 'Brest,' he exploded and waited for acknowledgement.

Supply teacher calmly continued correcting his work and without looking up, replied, 'Ah yes, French naval port, north-west France.'

Last week, not one morning was he on time for registration and when we told him to wash his hands, for he had just come

130

from a paper round, he coolly remarked, 'You know, I've come here to learn, not to be insulted.'

After two weeks I had a meeting with his head of house, his mother and his educational welfare officer, with Wonderboy present. I pulled no punches, said that I felt the lad needed more specialised help than I could give him, and it was agreed that we should approach the Tavistock Clinic for psychiatric support. Meanwhile, this week he was in on time every morning and took himself into the bathroom on arrival to wash his face and hands before going upstairs to the classroom. Perhaps we could do more for him than I had predicted.

The days passed, the fifth-years worked hard while the fourth-years enjoyed the weather and the garden. My own boys were growing up without me.

I received by first post one morning Christopher's application form for a provisional driving licence with cover note of one line – 'Please could you send this off with cheque'. I couldn't believe my eyes when the second post was shunted through my letter-box – a signed application form for Christopher's passport with a similar note, 'Please enclose cheque and send off to the Passport Office.' He was either preparing himself to flee the country or he was so bored with his school work that he had taken to completing bureaucratic forms to occupy his time. Whatever the reason it did appear to be at my expense, I noted.

Meanwhile I became worried about Wonderboy who, since his arrival here, hadn't put a foot wrong, and yesterday produced thirty-five pounds from his grubby pocket and informed us he was off to buy a crossbow. The child wasn't seen again and wasn't at registration next morning, and his mother hadn't a work number for me to check whether he'd shot himself with his own arrow. I cleared my conscience by ringing his educational welfare officer with all this information. It was called passing the buck.

Nick had managed to catch a cold and was croaking round the house. I first noticed it when I was closing the windows against the rain and wind, which had already broken the badminton net. I mentioned that Dog needed a walk and then remarked, 'Your voice is breaking.'

131

He gave me a stony stare and replied, 'Mother, you're really thick sometimes. My voice broke a year ago, I've got a stinking cold.' I felt suitably chastened and looked at Dog resignedly – he knew that the weather controlled whether he would join the long-distance walkers or whether it would be a zip-out, where he was expected to perform all functions simultaneously and zip back without rolling his eyes plaintively. I grunted my resentment, but pulled on my wellington boots to the ecstasy of Dog, who was now leaping round me like a demented wallaby. I rebuked him with a kick, which the brainless animal acknowledged as a form of endearment and wagged his bottom from side to side, not doubting that I was that trusting, loving human being who was his best friend.

It had been confirmed officially that ILEA would no longer financially support Project Spark after the next year. Typically, I was not informed of this decision – I had discovered it only by chance. I had received through the post a hundred-and-three-page document from ILEA called 'The Review of Off-Site Support Units'. I was leafing through it casually, when I came upon a table of support centres giving the current position of pupils and staffing capacity. Opposite this page was a table giving the proposed positions for the next year. Project Spark was mentioned under the current position, but to my horror it was not mentioned on the opposite table. I stared at it dumbfounded, desperately re-reading it in case I had made a mistake. We were simply not mentioned. We had been eradicated. I studied the two pages yet again. On the left page we were listed, on the right we were not.

I reached for the phone, shaking. If Spark closed down I should be out of a job and since the house went with the job, I should have to move. Where should I go? I had no capital to buy even the smallest property, my meagre salary was used up on my children's school fees. I suddenly felt terribly, terribly frightened.

She was very sorry, she said, but the divisional officer was out all day, could she take a message? I ached with anxiety as I replaced the receiver, unable to bring myself even to say thank you. I sat there in my chair, the same chair I had sat in for twelve years, hearing the problems of the Spark children. I rested my head back as I had done so many times before to listen to their dreams, their aspirations, their sorrows, their fulfilments and frustrations. Indeed, what would happen to the kids without our sort of provision? Dog pushed his nose into my lap and blew like a horse through his nostrils in sympathy and in that moment the sweet memories of Jake, my dead twelve-year-old junkie, fused into the present, bringing one agonising torment of utter failure, desolation and loneliness. It is a sad truth that those endowed with a deep well of love also are endowed with a deep capacity for suffering. It was a great darkness that descended, as did the night, upon my spirit.

Next morning I rang the head of the local comprehensive as soon as I could and asked him to come round. He arrived all jolly until I showed him the offending document. 'But I know nothing of this. No one's informed me that it's being closed down. It's preposterous. What will we do for our difficult children?' His astonishment was not an act, he seemed genuinely amazed that he had not been informed that his support unit was about to be axed. 'It must be a misprint,' he kept repeating. He rang his deputy head and insisted he drop everything and come round immediately.

He, too, ploughed through the document, only to splutter in astonishment. 'There must be a misunderstanding,' but I don't think any of us really believed it. 'My chairman of governors isn't going to like this,' he declared pompously. 'Indeed not,' acknowledged the deputy head. I felt as if I were in *Toad of Toad Hall* listening to them. 'Sally, I'm going to divisional office this afternoon for a meeting with secondary heads. I'll find out the facts and then we'll meet and decide on what action to take.' I felt defeated; if the powers that be had decided to close Spark down, what the hell could we do about it? 'I'll phone you,' he said as he left.

He did not phone me, so next day I rang the school. His secretary said he was in a meeting till midday, when he would contact me. Faithful Dog followed my pacings like a leech, getting nothing in return for his devoted trouble, not even a walk. Kind and loyal Dog stared into my eyes reproachfully, observing my pity turn to anger, and turn back again to pity.

The phone rang: yes, the head confirmed, ILEA were no longer prepared to finance Spark, but according to them they were not in a position to close it as it was a charity in its own right. Therefore only the trustees could officially close it down. He suggested we should call a meeting with the trustees and ILEA in the near future, but now he had to fly as he had a parent waiting.

I sat there alone with Dog, his head in my lap, with my tears gushing over his feathered ears. How dare they say *they* were not axing us, for they were only too aware that by withdrawing their financial support we could not continue. What about my position as an educational welfare officer? Do they redeploy me or make me redundant, for they cannot sack me? Above all, what I could not understand was that this arbitrary decision had been made by the hierarchy, with no discussions, no visit here to evaluate or assess the work we were doing, and with obviously no thought or care for what would happen to the children. I was torn by conflicting desires, one, to use all my strength and courage to fight this cruel injustice, the other, simply to resign myself to the inevitable and go and begin a new life elsewhere. Not so easily done in one's mid forties, I reminded myself.

The next morning the sun shone and my bowed spirit warmed to the light. I knew that whatever the links of the past to the present, my only weapon now lay in the future. Before the Spark kids arrived, I washed Nick's sweaters and hung them out to dry. The billowing clouds rolled over the blue skies and as the rain came down, yet again, I thought that suicide was cheaper and less hassle than emigration.

Wonderboy had returned all in one piece, sans crossbow, and joined three other Spark children on a day's school outing to Margate. Fortunately for them it was the day summer came and went all in twenty-four hours and I was to hear all the gossip next day from a teacher, who informed me that some of my kids had over thirty pounds in their pockets to spend during the outing. I could not believe it. One of my children spent twenty pounds on the fruit machines alone and then bought a pair of swimming trunks, so he could bathe in the sea. On coming out of the water, the teacher assured me, he buried the new costume in the sand because he could not be bothered to carry it home on the coach!

I had hardly noticed half-term with my preoccupation with the future of Spark. Chinese boys came and went. Masahide paid us a flying visit en route back to boarding school, having been on a school trip to Russia. I seemed to spend most of my time on the phone trying to organise an evening when all my trustees, head and deputy head, the chairman of governors and members of the ILEA hierarchy could meet. In fact, I had no idea what had gone on at half-term till well after the event.

Wonderboy had knocked on my door. 'Come in.' As soon as he entered I noticed a new sense of well-being about the lad. He was clean and well dressed in a somewhat unfashionable way. He was self-assured but no longer assuming an air of superiority. His cadaverous, good-looking face lit up as I turned round in my chair and greeted him. I liked his quiet and careful voice.

'I wondered if you have any spare batteries for my calculator?'

'No, I don't think I have. If you haven't a lesson in the next half hour, you can borrow my bike and I'll give you some money and you can pop round to the shops. You can get me some milk at the same time,' I added.

'No, sorry, that's no good. I have a maths lesson in school in ten minutes. Never mind, I'll manage without. It's not that important, but sorry about the milk.' He was about to depart when I had an idea.

'Hold on, Nick usually keeps spare batteries for his Walkman. I'll go and have a look in his room.' I pounded up the stairs, leaving Wonderboy hovering in the hall. I have never been the type of mother who constantly nags her children from morning to night about what I consider trivia, which is exactly how I regard housework. I am not a domesticated woman, but I do keep the house tidy, purely because it is convenient for me to do so, as I never know what time of day, and come to that, night, a parent, teacher, social worker, or policeman might turn up.

If the children wish to have a friend to stay, the unsaid rule is their room is cleared up and left visibly clean and tidy for their visitor, so occasionally at weekends there are blitzes, when the dustpan and brush and vacuum cleaner are briefly engaged. On the whole I do not venture into my children's rooms unless invited. I have always respected their privacy as I expect them to respect mine. But Nick was at school and I knew he would not mind my borrowing some batteries. Of course I had no idea where he kept them, so I began my search anti-clockwise. He has a desk for his art work, a desk for his computer, a table for his woodwork and a desk where he sits and does his homework. I tried all these to no avail, before I ventured to his bedside table and opened the small cupboard beneath the drawer. There, behind a row of torches and illegal flick knives, was a litre bottle of Smirnoff vodka. I forgot about the purpose of my search. I took the bottle out. It was only half full. The label, I noted, was in Russian. I unscrewed the top and took a swig. It was beautiful, pure, neat Russian vodka. Carefully I replaced the bottle, closed the cupboard door and went downstairs. 'I'm terribly sorry, out of luck, I couldn't find any batteries.'

'Never mind! I'd better go or I'll be late – see you later.' Wonderboy departed and I returned to my room and sat down in my chair, musing. Obviously, Masahide had sneaked it through Customs and the two of them had been having nocturnal orgies. Didn't have to be nocturnal now I came to think of it. I wondered how best to deal with this. There was no way I could confront the two of them together as Masahide was back at boarding school and a confrontation with Nick alone seemed not only unfair, but would predictably lead to a terrible row and days of not communicating thereafter. So I decided on a more subtle and passive approach. I returned upstairs and collected the bottle. Fortunately for me, my own bottle of vastly inferior vodka was only quarter full, sitting in my drinks cabinet. I poured the good Russian alcohol into my quarter-full bottle and then went to the kitchen and filled Nick's bottle half full of water, and with great care placed it back in his bedside cupboard. No words were to pass my lips on the subject till months later, when in the holidays Nick and Masahide were making shandies for Sunday lunch.

'I'm delighted to see you've both given up the spirits,' I announced casually. They looked sheepishly at one another and then Masahide bravely spoke up.

'I am most sorry, Sally, that was not good what I did,' he said in his almost-fluent English. He hesitated before daring to ask, 'Did you write to Japan and tell my father of this?'

I smiled, 'No, of course I didn't. I put it down to puberty. But I will, if it happens again.'

'It will never happen again,' he said seriously, and then looked up questioningly. 'What is puberty?'

'Growing-up, Masahide,' I replied lightly, and turned to my youngest son. 'And what about you, Nick? Have you learnt your lesson?'

He smiled a charming, serene smile and replied, 'Well, I know one thing I've learnt, if it ever does happen again I'll find a better place to hide it.' We all laughed, but for different reasons.

Chapter 15

Children do not have a monopoly on growing up. I believe for all of us life should be a continuous, conscientious growth towards enlightenment – or should I say truth, a word often used indiscriminately. I believe mind is fostered by mind and conscience is fostered by conscience. How can one learn to become a good painter or appreciate good art? One learns to paint by painting and one learns to appreciate art by going to art galleries and looking at pictures. I believe enlightenment results 'when knowledge of the world starts out from knowledge of men's souls'.

As a child, I was told how selfish and self-centred I was, and I learnt to fear and feel guilty of the word 'self-love'. I was ashamed and felt depreciated. It took me years to understand that those around me had got it all wrong; that this did not necessarily mean self-adulation, but pride and faith in the good potential within myself. I learnt to educate myself in increasing measure as I attained a deeper understanding of human beings and all that is human. Real enlightenment can only come from self-understanding. Often the truth about oneself can be bitter and unpleasant, but it should never debase human dignity, for self-respect promotes respect and awareness of others. Therefore, kindness and forgiveness are essential elements of self-truth.

I was guilty of many serious misdemeanours as a teenager, but I am convinced there were many occasions when forgiveness would have had a far more powerful moral impact on me than punishment ever did. After all, punishment, particularly when it may not be justified, just fills one with resentment and stunts all growth. I am not advocating that our sons and daughters should never have 'no' said to them and that under the banner of 'free expression' the little darlings should be allowed to do exactly what they like. I believe that discipline is as an essential ingredient as are kindness and forgiveness and that self-discipline is part of one's search for self-truth.

The vital essence in Project Spark was our ability to foster the right attitude to discipline, criticism and disapproval; all of which could be extremely negative influences upon the minds of our volatile children and sour them for life.

When Pat was sent to us he was such a case, who had been ground down to a pulp by his home life. He attended us erratically, was always late because he was too depressed to get out of bed, and had not a single friend. Pat's difficulties began and remained in his family. The tensions were considerable and the family were locked into themselves, and unable to communicate. Pat's parents were divorced and he lived with his mother and stepfather who, when they had time for him, were critical and disapproving. He always arrived silent, often dirty, and completely disorganised for he could no longer cope with everyday reality. Neither praise nor encouragement seemed to pierce his emotional barriers. We tried to foster positive attitudes within him, but his depression and indifference completely paralysed him to such an extent that he did not respond even to his own name.

An inhibited, depressed, self-loathing child cannot think or act normally. Equally, it is almost impossible to treat a child with sensitive awareness if one has no access to his emotions and no level of communication. This was very much the situation with the Spark staff and Pat. In fact, it was eighteen months after the event, that we discovered Pat's stepfather had left his mother, for which she blamed her son. Two years later we were to discover that Pat was seeing his real father, who at the time of the divorce was grievously embittered for not being given custody of his son, and was also blaming Pat for siding with his wife and not him. The child could do no right and, in self-defence, completely

140

switched off. We did consider care proceedings to remove him from this intolerable situation, but as the law stood we had no real grounds for committal. Pat remained with us for nearly three years and he remained an isolated, indifferent, depressed child whom, with all our love and experience, we could not help.

The entente cordiale between the oppressor ILEA and the victim, Project Spark, eventually took place in a calm but tense atmosphere one evening. Pleasantries were exchanged and cups of coffee served, despite the temptation to pour it all over them. Our chairman called the meeting to order and the divisional officer for ILEA plunged in by saying how much he appreciated our work.

'Got a fine way of showing it,' I muttered audibly and was given a warning look that would freeze a volcano, by our new chairman of trustees. I was ignored by the divisional officer, who was now informing us that he had approached County Hall with a view to persuading them that Spark should be classified as 'on site' rather than 'off site'; as it was policy to support on-site units they might reconsider our position. That appeared to be the good news, and the bad news followed. ILEA was no longer prepared to fund my position as an education welfare officer to Project Spark.

'What have I done to upset them?'

'No, you haven't understood. The educational welfare department is being restructured into certain teams dealing with certain districts and you cannot be spared to run Spark. You will have to become a member of a team.'

'But I am Spark,' I replied arrogantly. 'If I'm not here to run Spark, but sitting in an office pushing papers round, it'll have to close. You know that.' I felt angry.

'If you don't like it, you can resign. Can Project Spark possibly cover the funding for Sally?' he asked the trustees.

Our chairman said this was most unlikely since the burden of fund-raising fell to Sally and she had no scope to devote more time to it. There was another serious problem, he pointed out. The teacher in Spark for the last two terms was still employed on a supply basis and not on a permanent

141

basis. At this point the school governors interrupted by saying they were also concerned that a resolution which they had made at the beginning of the year for the Spark teacher to be appointed as a Scale 2 teacher had received no response from ILEA. I had to smile at that; six months had passed and they still had not replied to the school governors! I thought of Butch Cassidy and the Sundance Kid being chased across the length and breadth of America by the sheriff's posse and Butch turned to the Kid and said, 'Who are those people?' It was just the right question. Who were those people in ILEA who were making crucial decisions about people's lives, but didn't even have the courtesy to inform those concerned, nor reply to letters from school governors?

'Who are these people?' I demanded. 'Come on, I want some names.'

I was told to calm down by a trustee, who then pointed out to the ILEA representatives that if the essence of ILEA's proposals was to save costs it should be pointed out that many of the children previously catered for by Spark would probably end up in care, the cost of which vastly exceeded any saving that the closing of Spark would achieve.

'Of course children in care are not our department and do not come out of our finances.' So that argument was wasted.

'So could you tell me why my teacher is not on Scale 2 and is paid as a supply teacher?'

'I'm afraid all teaching positions were frozen some time ago. We're having to cut back.'

And so the evening progressed with no satisfactory answers and ample excuses. Finally, it was repeated that the ILEA development sub-committee had instigated a special investigation into the future of all voluntary bodies and that in connection with this they would visit Spark. I wanted to laugh. No one present realised that all this bureaucracy was a front for those political species who liked to feel important and hear their own voices, and that, in fact, nothing would be done. It was all a farce. When the ILEA people had departed the head and school governors shook hands warmly with my innocent trustees, saying what a good meeting it had been. I could have quite cheerfully kicked them all in the

142

teeth. Only I seemed to understand that Project Spark was doomed. One way or another, but without sacking me, we were to be closed.

As my chairman left he said, 'Don't be gloomy Sally, we got a long way this evening. I'm very optimistic. I think it might be an idea if we approach the Minister.' With this grand idea he departed also.

Spark was very quiet. The fifth-years were officially on exam leave, but virtually all of them came in. Freddy stayed on to work even in the evenings, for he had decided to go on to sixth-form college and try for university. It was lads like him who proved over and over again that there was a place for Spark in the educational system, for if he had never been sent to us, he would have become a drop-out.

I was taking the kids for English that day, as my teacher was checking how well the kids were doing on work experience. From the expression on her face on her return, I realised all was not well. 'You know Jack's supposed to have been working at Houghton Motors for one day a week – well, no one's seen him – he hasn't turned up once in the last four weeks and, do you know, the boy's been claiming travel expenses there and back.' I smiled to myself. Yet another kid working the system before he's out of nappies.

That evening Piers's stepfather phoned. It was five days before Piers was due to sit his final exams.

'Sally, I thought I ought to tell you, you won't be seeing Piers again.'

'I'm sorry. What do you mean?'

'I've got a job in Basingstoke and we're moving down there tomorrow.' I knew it must have been a very recent decision as Piers had not mentioned it to us.

'But what about Piers? He starts his exams next week.' I was aghast.

'Well, that's why I'm ringing you, he's coming with us, so he can't sit his exams.'

'But he must,' I cried passionately. Had the man gone completely off his head?

'Well he can't. He's got to come with us,' he replied,

143

somewhat aggressively. The man has lost his bloody marbles, I thought.

'Look, hold on. We've just spent five years educating this boy so that he can take and pass those exams. His whole future depends upon them. You can't just cut his future off like that.' I was in despair.

'I've got to think of my future – this is the first job I've been offered in two years. I'm taking it and moving tomorrow – they've offered us a house. It'll be good to get the kids and the wife away from London. There will be more opportunities for Piers down there.'

'Piers will be offered no opportunities if he hasn't got his exams,' I pointed out as calmly as I could.

'Well, he won't pass them. I got no education and I've got by.'

'He has a very good chance of passing them – please, please can you not rethink this one? Couldn't you wait three weeks when his exams are finished?'

'No way, I've accepted the position and it starts the day after tomorrow.' I started clutching at straws. 'What about his grandmother, couldn't he stay with her and join you later?'

'No, she's in hospital. She had her leg amputated yesterday.'

I didn't believe what I was hearing though I knew it had to be true, for Piers had told us that morning. 'I'm so sorry.' I knew I didn't sound it, but my thoughts were elsewhere.

'When she's better she'll come down and we'll look after her. She'll be alright.'

'I'm sure she will,' I muttered, as much to myself as to him.

'Sally I don't want you to think we're ungrateful for all you've done, but to be quite honest, this job is more important than some bloody old exams. Me and the missus have no exams and we're doing all right like.'

I knew I was wasting my breath, but for Piers's sake I had to find a solution.

'What about if I found a place for him to stay, would you agree to that?'

He hesitated. 'Well, I dunno about that. No, not in London on his own.'

I sensed victory. 'Oh no, I agree with you – not on his own, but what about if it was with someone you knew?'

'Well that's different, but I don't want him staying with his friends. He'd be out all night.' He paused, and then added, 'And I ain't got the wherewithal to pay for his food.'

I crossed my fingers and gave it my best shot. 'What about if I have Piers to stay here? I don't want any money for his keep and I'll see he's in every night by ten o'clock. You know he behaves well with us and I'll put him on the first train to Basingstoke after his last exam.' There was a very long pause.

'Would you be prepared to do that?' His voice had mellowed.

'Indeed I should – my kids would be thrilled and Dog would love it.'

So they went off to Hampshire and Piers came and stayed with us for three weeks. The old boy passed his exams and came and visited us some time later. His father was still employed down there and his mum and nan loved the countryside.

'And you Piers? What about you?' I asked. He grinned broadly.

'You should be proud of me Sal, I'm training to be a plumber.'

It was lunchtime. I had caught the bus over to Kensington to visit social services there. From the bus upstairs I saw my favourite Spark boy with a mate in a telephone booth. I looked at my watch, for precisely at that moment he should have been at an interview at Paddington College, to be accepted on a special bridging course whereby he would spend two days a week next year attending college. I was so upset that I leapt to my feet and ran down the aisle and furiously rang the bell to make the bus halt, even though it had not reached an official bus stop. I fell down the stairs as it turned the corner into another street and drew up, both driver and conductor looking somewhat puzzled. I hadn't time to explain, so jumped from the stationary vehicle and ran hell for leather back from where the bus had passed. If he had still been in the telephone booth I think I would have killed him, for only yesterday he had promised me faithfully that I didn't need to accompany him and that he was quite adult enough to get himself there. To think I had trusted the wretch; why don't I ever learn?

The lad appeared next morning bright eyed and bushy tailed. I was still burning with indignation.

'How did your interview go?'

'It was okay, Sally.' I just managed to contain myself from erupting and strangling the lying hound.

'What did you do after – go back to school?'

'No, me and a mate went home – wasn't worth going back to school.'

'No more than it was worth going to the college I suppose,' I suggested. He puckered his brow and appeared bewildered. It crossed my mind that he should do drama as part of next year's course, for this was becoming an Oscar-winning role. 'What yer mean?' he said.

'You bloody-well know what I mean. This time you've blown it boy.' The child stood quite still, looking down at me in stunned silence.

'What yer rabbiting on about Sal?'

'You cheat! How dare you come in here and lie to me? I trusted you.'

He flicked his hair back off his forehead and began to protest. 'I haven't lied to you. I don't know what you're talking about.'

'Where were you at midday yesterday?'

He thought about it for a very long second. 'I guess we were on our way home.'

'How could you be on your way home at that time, when your interview was then?' I cried triumphantly. He thought for another very long second, his eyes showing no comprehension, and then he had the audacity to smile.

'What the hell are you smiling for? You're in deep trouble,' I frothed.

'Sal, you've got it wrong. I did go to the college and got there an hour early and because the kid in front of me never showed up, they took me in for my interview early. Ring the college if you don't believe me,' he added as an afterthought. I was relieved, and angry with myself for having doubted him.

'I'm sorry. I thought after all the trouble we've taken to get you on this course you'd just done a bunk.' He grinned cheerfully and swept the hair away from his forehead yet again.

'Who? Me Sal? I wouldn't do that to you.'

Late afternoon my elderly trustees gathered here for a meeting. The main issue was, had I heard further from ILEA or the school governors? Nothing, I replied in an I-told-you-so-fashion. They pondered on this and then decided that the chairman's idea to write to the Minister should be the next course of action, and so they left me in peace and gloom.

Chapter 16

Our academic year began with the news that Wonderboy had fallen down a hole on a building site where he was trespassing. He had broken his hip and had spent the major part of the summer holidays confined to hospital. Minutes after this telephone message, my favourite Spark boy bounced in with the tragic news that one of my old boys had killed himself in a car crash the previous day. No other person involved. He was barely nineteen. He had come to us as a loud, tough, over-confident, pushy thirteen-year-old who disrupted the classroom by rolling on the floor in the middle of lessons. We had worked hard for him and now he was dead. All that time, all that concern, all those decisions, all that care wiped out just like that. I felt so negative that I couldn't face the Spark kids that morning, so I retired to the garage on my own and cleaned out the deep freeze.

Meanwhile, our fight for Spark was continuing in a bureaucratic, dreary, by-the-book fashion. My father, a trustee, had written to John Patten MP, Minister of State at the Home Office.

Project Spark is a prime example of partnership between the private and public sectors and its undoubted success over the years has had a direct bearing on the prevention of crime in the inner city areas – although admittedly, not on a large scale. The philosophy behind it could be applied, however, on a national scale. It is now under the threat of closure as a result of ILEA's proposed policy of withdrawing financial support to 'off-site' units. The chances of Project Spark surviving as a private charity alone are remote and in any case, the severing of the educational bonds between the school and the Project would completely negate one of the main objectives of the Project.

I shall be taking up the issue of education with Mr Kenneth Baker, but I am addressing this appeal to you as the Home Office Minister concerned with law and order. Close this Project down, and I can guarantee at least twelve additional claimants per term on police time, not to mention the cost of Magistrates' Courts and, in many cases, prisons and detention centres! Can you help in any way? I understand from Sally that she herself wrote to the Secretary to the Home Office, Mr Hurd . . .

I never received a reply from Mr Hurd, but Sir Peter Trench received one from Mr Patten at the Home Office:

. . . I can understand your concern, and your daughter's, that the Inner London Education Authority should be reducing their support for a project in which clearly a considerable amount of energy and personal commitment has been invested. I am sorry to have to tell you however that I do not think that the Home Office can help. The problem of disruptive children of school-age is primarily a responsibility of the local education authority and, at Government level, the Department of Education and Science.

. . . You probably know that Sally's letter to Douglas Hurd has already been forwarded to the Department of Education and Science. To complete the picture I am copying this letter and yours to Kenneth Baker . . .

I never received acknowledgment of my letter from the Department of Education and Science, but titled Sir Peter did, and from the Minister herself, Angela Rumbold. She, too, was unable to intervene on the Project's behalf.

Immediately, I re-read Kenneth Baker's proposed Education Bill to see what provision was being made for my

150

type of child. There was none, apart from a suggestion that some children might be exempted from the proposed tests at seven, eleven and fourteen years old, which would give no child a further chance. I knew at the time that there was now virtually no chance of stopping the closure of Spark. However much we were needed, however successful we had been or could be, was totally irrelevant. The hangman, whether we were innocent or guilty, would see us at the gallows.

Despite the obvious fate of Spark, I was asked to take another lad. I have nicknamed him 'Tiny' as he was such a little fellow for fifteen. He had a long history of school problems which was not surprising considering his family were homeless and were being shunted from one hotel or bed-and-breakfast accommodation to another, while they were waiting to be rehoused. At the end of the day in Spark, he had to ring his hotel to see if his family were still there or if they had been moved on, so we were his only security at present and this was the only reason I agreed we should take him. It was not fair to take on new kids, whom I should not be able to see through to their school-leaving age. Imagine if I suddenly turned round on them one morning and said 'Sorry mates, because of policy nobody's prepared to finance Spark any longer, so you can't ever come here again after today.' I had even thought of trying to raise the money privately, but ILEA closed that avenue by saying they wouldn't send children to me unless an ILEA teacher was employed and I was ILEA supported.

My new fifteen-year-old Spark girl had me really worried. I could smell evil when she entered the room. I had met it twice before in my life and each time the people concerned had been totally amoral. One ended up with a life sentence and the other was condemned to a notorious secure mental hospital. When the child's mother was explaining to me that her daughter had tried to kill her younger sister, the child began to laugh; not an embarrassed titter, but a gleeful devilish roar. The previous weekend, after a tiff with her parents, she locked herself in the bathroom and began to mutilate herself, beginning by making her nose bleed. She had bunked off school every morning and nobody knew where she went – she drifted home around ten at night, and one weekend was missing over twenty-four hours.

I felt uneasy for there was a turbulence that was sinister. I thought it was time to ask for help. I rang the social services and spoke to the duty officer. I hoped they'd go round and visit. I also arranged to see the educational psychologist the following week about the girl, but really I felt she needed a psychiatrist. I felt I had never met anyone so consumed with hate. My instinct was to be proved right yet again.

My Spark teacher arrived, all breathless, to say that a fourth-year kid had approached her in school to inform her that the Spark girl was visiting a fifty-year-old man down the road. Last week he had bought her shoes and given her fifteen pounds. I rang the social services and was informed that the social worker dealing with the Spark girl case was on leave. Unfortunately though, I could not speak to the duty officer as she was interviewing. I slammed down the receiver.

I decided to visit the local police station: I was shown into a dirty, smoke-ridden little room the size of a toilet, where I told my woeful tale. 'Ah, complications there!' my friendly man in blue said. 'You see, if this man lives in Maxter Terrace, it's not on our patch. You'll have to go to Golders Green.' I stared stupidly at the poor man.

'You're not going to do anything?'

He spread out his hands despairingly. 'Can't very well when it's not on our patch. Best thing you can do is go to the police station at Golders Green,' he reiterated.

Banging the door behind me, I drove to Golders Green where I repeated my fears for the Spark girl.

On my arrival home my teacher decided to show me exactly where this old boy lived. It was at the back of a nearby estate overlooking washing lines and a dumping ground. Not a salubrious area. I played detective, keeping my distance so as not to be seen, when three CID and a uniformed policewoman arrived. I pointed out the offending flat and went home. Two hours later the sergeant from Golders Green police station rang to say that the Spark girl was indeed found there and that all occupants of the flat were now being interviewed at the police station. Meanwhile, would I kindly get in touch with the mother as I already knew her? How does one break that sort of news, to an already distraught woman, over the phone? I had only managed to relate half the story when the receiver clattered to the floor and the weeping and wailing of a totally distressed lady echoed down the line. Someone at the other end picked up the phone and I quietly explained that the mum must ring Golders Green police station. Like a coward I then terminated the call.

I knew I should have offered to meet the mum and take her to the police station. To deal with such a delicate matter over the telephone was quite unforgivable. How could I have been so obtuse? Was it laziness? Or was I just losing heart? Was the fight for Spark burning me up, diminishing my enthusiasm and caring qualities? If that was the case, then perhaps it *was* time to close Spark, I thought.

As the days passed, further calls came from police, social services and the mother. At least we had activated some concern for the child, but whether anyone would actually make any decisions or take any action was another matter altogether. I doubted it. The mother rang to tell me that the old man had contacted her and had agreed to meet with the parents. She begged me to be present. What good could come from such a meeting, I wondered?

I had a very positive meeting with the educational psychologist about the Spark girl. She seemed to grasp the immediacy of our problems with this very disturbed child and, while I was present, rang the social services to see what action was being taken. She could not get through. Later in the afternoon, they rang to inform me that they would try to make an appointment for next week to see the family. Infuriated with their lack of pace, I asked why the matter couldn't be dealt with today. 'It's Friday,' was the reply, which was apparently meant to placate me. I hadn't the energy to reiterate that I had in fact rung them over a week ago to ask them to visit.

So that evening I phoned the mum to say the social services would be contacting her the next week, for I didn't want her to think that she had no support or help. I also told her that

I had had second thoughts about the meeting with the old man next Monday.

'Funny you should mention him, he rang us last night and he was very drunk.' Another good reason not to meet, I thought, so I finally advised her that she should inform the police of this meeting and the phone calls and that I would not be present.

Meanwhile, Tiny was settling in well. One morning he came with the news that his family would be rehoused within the year – that is if Nobby was put away. Nobby turned out to be his younger brother, but not the youngest. 'Funny,' he said, 'it's always the middle one that's difficult. My auntie has three and it's her middle one that's just like Nobby.'

'How old is Nobby?' I asked.

'Thirteen, but Dad says no one will give us a home as long as Nobby's with us,' he replied with such resignation that I believed him. Of course nobody would rehouse them if Nobby the Terrible, aged thirteen, wasn't put away.

Chapter 17

Dog was first taken ill on a Wednesday – by ill, I mean he didn't eat his supper. On the heath next day he wasn't interested in chasing either the rabbits or the squirrels. He lay around lethargic and dull-eyed and again wouldn't touch his food. As I caressed him I felt his glands all swollen round his neck and realised he really wasn't at all well. I was busy with supper that evening as we had three extra Overseas Educational Services children in the house for their half-term, so Nick kindly offered to take him to the vet. On his return he reported that Dog had been given an antibiotic injection and that his temperature was 104 degrees.

For the next three days, daily visits to the vet for further injections brought down his temperature, but not his swollen glands. He obviously found it difficult to swallow and continued to be uninterested in whatever I offered him to eat. On Monday I took him round to the surgery and voiced my worries. The vet agreed that he wasn't responding as he should and eventually said, 'I think we'd better have him in and have a look inside.' Dog glanced at me reproachfully with his tail weakly thumping the floor.

'We're going to get you better,' I promised my faithful hound. He was given a sleep-inducing injection and I carried him gently to the operating table. 'See you later, old boy.' I stroked him, and went home to continue my day in Spark, the vet having promised to ring me at lunchtime.

Only half an hour later the telephone rang. It was the vet. 'I'm afraid it's not good news. He has leukaemia – his lymphatic glands are cancerous and I feel I have no alternative but to put him to sleep.' I heard a squeak erupt from my vocal chords and like a fountain turned on, the tears began to fall. He was only seven and had never had a day's illness in his life. Till last Wednesday he was chasing everything with his unequalled enthusiasm and exuberance. How would I break the news to Nick and Christopher who were as devoted to him as I was? He wasn't a dog, he was part of the family, a major consideration in all our lives. My walks with him had been a daily ritual for seven years.

'Oh God, no,' I howled aloud to anyone that would listen to me. The house would never be the same without him. He was put down, having never woken from the anaesthetic, at eleven that morning. I sat miserable and red-eyed by the telephone, finding it difficult to comprehend that an hour ago my friend had pushed his wet nose into my hand for reassurance and now he was dead. I cried all day. I rang Christopher with the news; he wept down the phone. As soon as Nick returned from school, I threw my arms round him and we cried together. We sat all evening, wringing out our handkerchiefs in turn. What Masahide from Japan thought, where no doubt dog was a gourmet's delicacy, I dreaded to think.

The passing away of a friend, even a four-legged one, leaves an emptiness of spirit and a pitiful loneliness. One is just left with cruel reminders – his bean bag in the kitchen, flattened in the middle where his sick body had curled up and lain in sleep. His leather lead hanging over the wall, waiting to be used for the next excursion to the heath, his dog bowl with his name on it, yesterday's water gathering a thin layer of dust as I hadn't bothered to re-place it with fresh, now that he had crossed his merciful boundary.

I had started a course in Aids counselling and I attended that evening; providential or fortuitous, the lecture was on 'Death and Bereavement'! I was the only member of the group who had not had a friend die of Aids. I could not bring myself to tell them that my best friend had died, for he was only a dog.

The season brought no further news of when Spark would close and we carried on, ignoring the possibilities. Two new intakes livened up the schoolroom.

Fatso waddled in on his first day and told me with gravity that his brain didn't need fodder, only his stomach; the second lad looked familiar.

'Don't I know you?'

'Nah, but yer know my bruvver – 'e were 'ere five years ago.' He looked me straight in the eye and observed me with laconic contempt. I jumped straight in.

'Do you know why you've been sent here?'

'Yeah.' It tripped off his tongue thoughtlessly.

'Good, then we won't waste each other's time. The schoolroom is upstairs on the left.' I turned to my desk and pretended to bury myself in my paperwork. He stood up, hesitant, the confidence had ebbed. I paid him no attention as he hovered and then he swivelled his bean-pole body through the door and leapt up the stairs two at a time. I had sensed a lot of energy there and unwittingly he had sharpened my own awareness of the lack of mine. Indeed, I was feeling so weary by the end of the school day that going out in the evenings was a major effort of will power. I was determined to complete my Aids course and attend the weekly lectures, but it became less enjoyable as the winter proceeded, though there was one exception.

One evening we had been divided into couples and for the first half-hour we had to practise our counselling skills with our partner. On this occasion my other half was Greg, who was the most devastatingly beautiful young homosexual with a porcelain face and watery eyes, the colour of Mediterranean sky. His gestures were curiously childlike and gentle and there was a stillness of such tenderness, that I wilted under his quiet gaze. I was quite riveted by his beauty and when during our co-counselling session he poured out his heart about the terrible row he had had the night before with his loved one, who then proceeded to pack his case and leave, my eyes had become equally watery. I could not help but reflect that if I had been his lover, I would never have got out of bed night or day.

Arriving home late at night after these sessions were the moments that I missed Dog the most. When I came through the front door there was no rapturous welcome, no beating of the tail, no irritating yelping of ecstasy in greeting, followed by a recalcitrant silence at my swears of annoyance and then that deep sigh of unconditional love as his wet nose nudged affectionately into one's crotch. I had never been able to persuade Dog from this habit, but, as Nick once said, it must be like smelling perfume to them. I was quite glad to finish the course on Aids in spring and be able to offer my services to the local hospital.

It was not long after this that my wallet was taken off my desk. It had a hundred pounds in cash and cheques worth two hundred and fifty in it. The Spark kids were the obvious suspects, but both my teacher and I found it hard to believe – or perhaps it just suited us not to believe it. I interviewed the children individually telling them the facts, neither with accusation nor blame, but they were dreadfully upset by the episode. So was I, for I felt so guilty and stupid for leaving it there in the first place.

'Of course it could have been the British Telecom man,' someone said.

'What British Telecom man?' I asked in surprise.

'The one I let in the other day to mend your phone.'

So the riddle was solved, for I knew perfectly well that my phone was not out of order. I put it down to experience.

We all sat in an unfriendly circle in the drawing-room with empty coffee mugs, as the divisional officer confirmed that ILEA would no longer financially support Spark after July, the end of the academic year. Once again he emphasised that as Spark was a charity in its own right only the trustees could close it. As for me, employed by the educational welfare department, I should have to be redeployed or resign. It was so strange to hear it. I had thought and spoken about it so much that it had seemed it would never happen. Yet I had expected it, especially after the recent announcement that ILEA was to be abolished in two years. However much one braced oneself and dared to hope, the words of truth were no less bitter. The endless talking was over. The light of Spark was to be blown out.

The days and weeks that followed were oppressive. My teacher was busy looking for a new job and when she had interviews I took the children. I had made the decision, rightly or wrongly, to say nothing to them for the present, but they watched me brooding and were graciously quiet and co-operative as if not to disturb my thoughts. It was as if each of us sensed in the other a sympathetic ally even though they were bewildered by their lack of understanding. I could not bring myself to tell them that our fight for the right to exist was over, that in a few months there would be nobody to take care of them or defend them; that even I should soon be abandoning them. How could I explain to them what I didn't comprehend myself, that we had been crushed out of existence not by a tangible enemy but by an intangible force called 'policy'?

Wretchedly, I continued my routine as director of Spark. One morning I was in school for an assembly of the staff to be addressed by the head. Someone mentioned he was out on a course for the week, and a teacher in a loud voice for all to hear, said, 'Is that why everything is running so smoothly for once?' The deputy head, standing not ten feet away, could not have failed to hear the remark, though chose to ignore it, and suddenly I realised how privileged my small project was without all the back-biters, staff-room jealousies and petty internal politics.

We never did hear what happened to our Spark girl, who by this time was no longer attending. The social services asked me to write a report, which I duly did; the psychologist asked me to write a report, which I did; and the police appeared twice more to interview me. Then silence. In the past I should have followed the family up, but in my inner world of black submission and balancing on the edge of such bleakness, I could no more help them than I could help myself.

Meanwhile, Jill had been sent to us. At least, she had been recommended and I had met her and it was agreed she should start in Spark at the beginning of the previous term, but she never appeared. I allowed a few days to pass and then daily rang her home, never to be rewarded with an answer. Eventually I pottered into school and talked to her mates and discovered where her mum was working. I rang her employer, only to be informed that they were still on holiday in Portugal! No longer was I amazed by the amount of international travel my children were provided with, yet they were all on free dinners. I had not forgotten the time when one of my children, also on free meals, was going on a ski-ing trip and his social worker asked ILEA for a grant to pay for his ski outfit – they gave it to him.

Jill eventually arrived back from the sun all bronzed and beautiful and occasionally turned up for lessons in school and more occasionally put in an appearance in Spark. She was a bright child, whose repartee could cut like a pair of sharp scissors through comments before they were completed. Her contemporaries in Spark were like fodder to a viper – and she was as slippery a one as I had had the misfortune to cross in many years. In frustration I rang her mother, who was quick to tell me that after giving birth to three boys she had been overjoyed to have a daughter . . . but now she had changed her mind, she was desperate for help. The boys had never been wild or so secretive. She couldn't understand why Jill was so difficult. I decided to put my little snake on report to be monitored by every teacher every hour of the day. Meanwhile, the mother, who appeared to think she had found an ally, rang me twice daily with evening and early morning behaviour bulletins. School rang to inform me she had been sent to the deputy head for spitting on a teacher, another morning she punched a girl in the face, breaking her glasses.

It was time for school, Spark and Mother to meet. I had the kettle simmering ready to make coffee, when Jill's mother rang to say that she wasn't coming and that she had decided to take Jill away and send her to live with her grandmother in the country from where she would attend the local school. It was an easy solution for Mother, Spark and school, but I doubted whether it would be for either Jill or grandmother. I was pleased the child was being offered a second chance for I had always suspected that she was acting up to the expectation of her peers and that she was now trapped in her 'naughty girl' image. If that was the case, her mother had made the right decision, but I couldn't help noting that we had notched up another failure of the feline species.

The loss of Jill, though a small part of daily life, added to my sense of impotence and apprehension. I felt suspended in a sleeping body, half struggling, half willing to be broken by my yoke of failure. But then, like a drowning animal with nostrils lifted, I would struggle to the surface and dizzily desire air and open my eyes and see that not all was bad. One morning I received the most encouraging letter from an employer of one of our lads on work experience, commending him for his timekeeping, willingness to do anything and his good manners. The employer wanted me to know that he was going to offer the boy a full-time placement with him when he left school in three months. I remembered when the child, aged fourteen, first came to us as a non-attender with behaviour problems and now he was about to sit five GCEs, which he would pass, and already had a job waiting for him. It did make Spark worth while and all these past years a significant contribution to the quality of life.

I wrote to the boy's employer a few days later, to thank him, and as I was posting the letter I met one of my former fellow dog walkers.

'I haven't seen you around for some time?' he said.

'No, I haven't been around. We lost Dog a month ago,' I replied tormentedly. I saw tears spring to his eyes and a turmoil of physical feeling blushed through his pale cheeks.

We had hardly known each other, in fact I don't think we had ever pursued a conversation beyond the weather, so his reaction quite stunned me and I hastily added, 'He didn't suffer long. It was all very quick.' I tried to soothe him as the tears poured down his cold, chiselled face. 'I'm so sorry, I didn't realise it would upset you so much.' I was more than astonished. He pulled out a handkerchief and swabbed his face.

'I'm so sorry, I'm so sorry. You've misunderstood. I lost my wife a month ago. We had been together forty-four years. I'm so sorry.' At that moment I felt I knew all that passed within him and the magnitude of what was left unsaid, as we nodded as one and parted.

Suffering is relative, but nevertheless it is a true condition of life. As I walked back, out of the corner of my eye I saw one of the Spark boys who should have been in a lesson in school. I waved to him and involuntarily he returned the wave, when it suddenly dawned on him that I had caught him bunking and he hastily lowered his head and looked sheepish, waiting to see what I would now do about it. 'You dick-head,' I muttered to myself, and turned my back upon the errant child. My sadness had conveyed me back to my damnable inertia.

It was three weeks before the end of term and we were having our bi-weekly support meeting at Spark. The deputy head and head of special education were present, my teacher was not. Now that it was common knowledge among the school staff that Spark was to close there was a curious atmosphere at these get-togethers. The warmth of sharing our dilemmas and ventures had turned to a sterile politeness. I could no longer conceal my wounds and they could no longer bridge the past and the present. We all recognised the futility of talking about the problems of the children when by the end of next term there would be no children. We had been meeting for twelve years, it was a ritual, so here we were again casting sidelong glances at one another drinking coffee and, for my part, with nothing to say. The head of special education, Mary, was a diminutive, intelligent woman who was absorbed totally by her work with difficult children. I had always liked her and respected her professionalism, but now as I lifted my head and looked at her tense face, I felt only acrimony. Something had come between us.

'Sally, did you know the teacher in our unit for eleven-to-fourteen-year-olds is moving to the maths department next term?' she began.

'No,' I replied truthfully, and reflected nostalgically on past days when it would have been called Spark One – not the unit.

'Well, she is and that leaves a teaching post available there.' I noticed the corners of Mary's lips tighten. She was dreadfully pale.

'So what are you going to do at such short notice – close it?'

'No,' she replied haltingly. 'We're going to advertise the position.'

'You're unlikely to get anyone. After all, any good teacher is in a job and has to give a half-term's notice.' I pointed out the obvious. The deputy head picked at his teeth and shuffled his feet uncomfortably.

'That may be so, but I thought you ought to know we've asked your teacher to apply for the position. They'll be interviewing at the end of term hoping that the person will start in the unit at the beginning of next term.' She watched me, her eyes crinkling up in concern, her mousy hair falling round her like a child's.

I was devastated. These people, whom I had regarded as my friends, had concocted this conspiracy behind my back.

'Thank you for letting me know. I'm sorry my teacher didn't have the guts to tell me, nor the head come to that. In fact I'm plain sorry. Please see yourselves out.'

'The children, if she gets the job . . .' she began, with the innocence of a freshly-laid egg. I turned, trembling with anger, only just in control of myself.

'If she gets the job . . .' I repeated sarcastically. 'If? Don't bloody try and con me. It's a set-up. Sure, you'll go through the procedure of interviewing, but I bet you a million to one she'll get it. As for the children . . . you care about them as much as you stir my sense of immorality. Now, please go.' They left and I sat there with my eyes shut.

The next morning I went into school to see the head to discuss the imminent departure of my teacher.

'Of course she'll get the post, so what contingency plans do you suggest we deploy for Spark next term?' I asked directly and stiffly.

'Oh, I wouldn't be so sure she'll get it. If there's a black candidate the governors will choose her in preference. Now I must fly, I'm teaching this period.' He raced away. This once,

163

I knew, just this once, if a black lesbian scientologist with one leg was to offer her services, she would not get the position, which I could never have been so sure of before. The candle of Spark was to die earlier than anyone had prepared for, and within its darkness was destroyed my own claim for a better world and a more caring society.

Chapter 18

On the first day of term I trundled into school prepared for the worst. I got more than I could have reasonably expected. Surprise, surprise, my teacher had been appointed to the unit, but the second blow was that all teaching posts in ILEA had been frozen from the end of last term. Whether the head or deputy head knew of this beforehand I shall never know, but it now meant that I was teacherless, and without a qualified ILEA teacher Project Spark could not function as an educational establishment. The school had informed the children and were giving them special timetables till they took their final exams in June when they left.

Spark had been quietly strangled without a single bleat. I left the school for the last time, unnoticed and with no farewells. I had given the place over twelve years' service. I walked home, my movements slow and heavy, like an old, weary carthorse under a load. I let myself into the house that had been a sanctuary for so many, and listened to the silence. I was defeated. The system had beaten Spark, but I knew in my heart of hearts it couldn't crush our spirit. I believed that spirit would live on.

I called a trustee meeting and informed them of my capitulation. I think my submission surprised them, but they could do nothing but accept it. Eighteen years of my life I had given to Spark and I was exhausted and emotionally drained. I felt an estrangement, a coldness. My defiance, my guilt, my desire to assume my part of responsibility in the human race had been swallowed up in the fight for survival. I had nothing left to give. We continued to sit, they in their pinstripe suits and uncluttered lives of business, and myself, fast receding from them in a blur, floating away as an irreconcilable stranger.

'You realise we have a commitment to the public – those that have sent money over the years. Those that have supported Spark financially,' the chairman was saying, and so they began to discuss their code of behaviour and their principles involved as trustees and how much capital the charity had and . . . I drifted in my no-man's-land of sadness and self-blame.

'Sally, what is your position now?' the chairman was addressing me.

'I shall resign from ILEA as an educational welfare officer,' I replied tonelessly, then added, 'I need time.' It had flashed out without warning. I had not thought about it. 'I need time,' I repeated, as much to myself as to those present in the room. A kind of excitement of getting to grips with reality went through me. 'I want a sabbatical. In most educational establishments one gets a term off after every seven years – please, can I stay here in the house till I've sorted myself out?' For, indeed, there was much to sort out as I had no capital and Nick was doing well at public school locally, so any move would have to be considered with his future in mind. My request was mulled over for another hour and finally they agreed to a sabbatical; for the present I could remain in the house. I had preserved some temporary security for myself and my sons.

No one looked in on my solitude for the next few months. The time melted away listlessly. The school caretaker organised the removal of the school furniture and Nick and I painted the schoolroom. For the first time for eight years I could have a bedroom and move out of the drawing-room. There were no phone calls from the school; an absolute silence. The Spark children must have felt betrayed for they never came round. Occasionally an old boy would turn up and express astonishment at its closure, but accepted its occlusion as commonplace.

Days were spent going through the filing cabinets and

discarding case files and reports and I packed up sacks of books and sent them round to the special education department of the school. Despite this obscure detachment as I went about my daily routine of clearing out the remnants of Spark, a slow corrosive guilt, as amorphous as the air we breathe, devoured me. I dared not look at the future. How I was to earn my living or keep the boys at school or where I was to live were like an obscure pain that crossed my mirror only when I chose to glimpse in it.

Half-term was once more upon me and I took the car to Waterloo Station to meet Masahide. I caught sight of him making his way through the crowds at the ticket barrier. He waved and I responded accordingly. He came up to me and kissed me warmly. Such a change from two years ago when he would greet me, Japanese style, with a stiff bow. I was about to turn to go to the car when he plucked my arm. 'Ha, Sally, please wait. There is small problem,' he explained, ever courteously. 'I have classmate with nowhere to go, so I said he come with us.'

'What do you mean exactly, he has nowhere to go? Hasn't he a family?'

'He foreigner like me. He come from Hong Kong – Chinese family back home and he no place to stay. He have to find bed and breakfast.'

I was wrestling with thoughts such as whether the weekend joint was big enough, and disbelief that the school would allow a sixteen-year-old Chinese loose in London wandering round b-and-bs.

'Where is this mate of yours?' Masahide pointed to his left and my little refugee was standing there with a body resembling Frank Bruno and a smile like a zebra crossing, every other tooth missing.

'He very excellent rugby player,' Masahide exclaimed with some awe.

'I'm sure,' I replied, my mild affirmation a reflection of my own curiosity. 'How old is he?'

'He my classmate. Like me he sixteen. This be first term at school in England. Never played rugger before. He excellent, Sally. I told him you have him. His name Wia Li.'

I was grabbed by a mallet-like hand and told how kind I was. Masahide stood there beaming, delighted with the success of his diplomatic coup d'état. So Wia Li, the giant, came home, too. It is somehow acceptable, or at least expected, that children from lower-class families are often neglected. The school had rung Wia Li's family to say that they felt it was unacceptable for Wia Li to spend ten days on half-term on his own in London in b-and-bs, but the father replied that his son was a big boy now and must take care of himself.

All credit to Wia Li, who seemed quite unperturbed but, let's face it, ignorance and innocence are a great substitute for courage. Having never been to London before he would most likely have lost all three in ten days. Masahide might not be fluent in English as yet, but he had taken on board the philosophy of Spark, which pervaded the house and all our actions in it. I was glad of his faith in me, especially now that I had so little in myself.

One morning when I was working on my curriculum vitae and wondering where the hell I was going to send it, I heard the post. There was only one letter and I noticed the Yorkshire postmark. It was from the deputy head of Beckenbrough School in Thirsk asking me if he could come to London to meet me. Andy Gray arrived the next morning at midday. Over lunch he gave me the background to Beckenbrough.

It was a residential 'special' school, founded in 1936. It was a charitable trust managed by the Quakers and officers of North Yorkshire, Cleveland, Leeds and Lancashire education authorities. Boys came to the school through the provisions of the Education Act 1981 and all fees were paid by their respective local education authorities. There were some forty boys on the roll, aged from nine to sixteen, all of whom had been assessed by an educational psychologist as being 'emotionally and behaviourally disturbed'. In addition they were all of above average intelligence and all had exceptional verbal abilities. Some were 'gifted'.

The school received regular placements from approximately twenty 'user' authorities and currently had an annual budget in excess of five hundred thousand pounds. The school building itself was an impressive Jacobean mansion to which purpose-built accommodation had been added. The current staffing of teachers was supported by care staff and a large domestic and administrative team; in addition the school employed its own social worker, consultant psychologist and after-care officer. A wide variety of subjects were taught to GCSE level. Some pupils were engaged in academic work two or three years ahead of the expected level for their age group. Boys were encouraged in any individual interest they might want to pursue and, indeed, often demonstrated their enormous potential in this way.

Beckenbrough's aim was to raise the level of their children's self-awareness. It was largely through the careful use of language that their kids were made aware of the possibility of change from fixed, narrow and often aggressive stances to negotiated relationships. This was taught by adult example and reasoned discussion directed towards encouraging the child to perceive the general principles underlying the actions of everyday life. Andy went on to say that in all this work they encouraged the highest standards in every part of a child's life in the certain knowledge that low expectations lead to low achievement.

A typical Beckenbrough candidate would not necessarily be delinquent, but was likely to be eccentric and difficult in his behaviour and certainly unable to fit into mainstream education. He would be bright, but likely to be under-achieving. By their very nature, boys from the school found it difficult adjusting to life in a large and generally unsympathetic community when they had to leave school after their GCSEs. The emotional development of disturbed children often took longer than that of an 'ordinary' child. Alas, continued Andy, the education system did not take notice of this need and some Beckenbrough boys found themselves 'drowning' rapidly when thrown into a 'sink or swim' situation on their departure from residential school. Many had fragile home lives, some had none. Some were in the care of their local authority.

'Take Osborne, who left Beckenbrough last summer, having been with us for four years. He was originally taken into care by social services, having witnessed his father murder his mother. He left us with seven O-levels and joined the sixth form of a school in his home town. He lived with what was to prove to be the last in a long line of foster placements. Osborne was asked to leave this school due to "lack of effort" at the same time as his foster placement collapsed. He's now living in a hostel, is excluded from or is unable to cope with any social network he knows, and has recently been involved with the police concerning petty theft.

'Now this case is not exceptional. The string of boys who leave us with good academic prospects but collapse due to lack of a caring professional support system is long and it happens every year.' I had been there, I knew it all too well. 'In short, the headmaster and I want to establish an on-going provision for our boys leaving Beckenbrough. We're convinced that given the right support at this point in their lives, many of our kids who do not succeed would otherwise do so. After all, we are looking after a group of boys of university calibre.' I nodded in agreement. 'Well, we became aware of your work down here in London with the Spark Two Project, providing support and care for pupils who are difficult, but exam-orientated and preparing to enter employment. Well, it became clear to us that Project Spark possessed the professional skills to meet Beckenbrough's need.'

I stared at the maniac dumbfounded. He blinked behind his glasses at me. I slowly found my words. 'First, I must inform you Spark Two has closed down. Second, there is only myself left and I'm not professionally qualified in anything. Third, where's the money going to come from to pay for it all? Spark has no more than what this house is worth.'

'Yes, I realise that is a problem. We should have to raise it.'

'How?'

'Industry might be interested considering the sort of lad we're dealing with, or educational trusts – you probably know more about it than I do as you've been raising money for years for Project Spark.'

'Indeed I have and it's a soul-destroying task,' I interrupted hastily.

'Look, I've got to get back to Yorkshire, my train leaves

in an hour. Will you think it over and give me a ring? No, better still, will you come up to Beckenbrough and talk to the head and see our work?' I had nothing to lose.

'Okay. I'll come up for a week. Meanwhile, I will report this conversation to my trustees and put them in the picture. Incidentally, does your management committee know you've approached us?'

'No, only the headmaster.'

'So you haven't got the official tag of approval even?'

'No, the head and I just wanted to know if you are interested.'

'I'm interested. I'll come up next month.' That was to be our first of many encounters and nights of discussions well into the dawn. Perhaps this was to be the future of Spark.

I visited Beckenbrough School as promised, and became more and more convinced that the need for a post-Beckenbrough unit, similar to a half-way house, perceived by Andy and the headmaster, was essential to the growth of these very bright children. I was convinced also that such an innovation was along the lines of Spark's philosophy. Together we did our sums. To buy a building to cater for up to ten children and staff and run it for five years would cost a million pounds.

'That's one hell of a lot of money to raise,' I commented dryly.

'Not if we halve it. If Spark sells the London house and we can persuade the local education authorities to contribute something towards the children's education, then you only have five hundred thousand pounds to raise.'

'And what happens after five years?'

'When we've proved it's successful, it'll become self-funding.'

'How?' asked the headmaster.

'Our aim is that the project be partly self-funded by year four and fully by year five, through fees paid by the local education authorities to place boys. All we need to find are ten sponsors each prepared to give fifty thousand pounds over a five-year period.' Andy's enthusiasm always made everything sound so simple.

'First we need to write a report explaining the needs and

171

putting forth our proposals and giving a breakdown of how we would run and finance it. I've got to have something on paper to give to the sponsors,' I said.

'Fine, so let's write a report.'

'Second, I want the project properly monitored, preferably by the National Foundation for Education Research, for this project could have enormous influence over the future of post-sixteen provision for disturbed pupils.'

'Okay, I'll go and see John,' offered Andy. Dr John Harland, senior research officer of NFER was just down the road at York University.

'Great! But I must repeat to you that at present nothing is official. When we've produced the report I will put it up for official approval before my trustees and only if they give their seal of approval shall we be in business. Now I must return to London.'

My next visit to Beckenbrough to join the headmaster and Andy for a long weekend to write our report, 'A Spark for the Future', was notable not for what happened in the north, but what happened in London in my absence.

Since Christmas, I had noticed pink letters in pink envelopes arriving as regularly as the daily milk bottles for Nicholas, who was now almost fifteen. I presumed they were from Annie, whom he had met in the holidays while he was staying in Yorkshire, but who attended boarding school in Dorset. I had known the family for some years, long before they left the metropolis in preference for the Yorkshire Dales, and it was a blessing in disguise for I stayed with them on my visits to Beckenbrough. This was unbeknown to my youngest. Before I left on the Thursday night, I went through the weekend's menus that I had cooked and prepared with Nick. 'Okay, all your meals are prepared. You've just got to turn on the oven.' He nodded his understanding. 'Now Nick what are you doing this weekend?'

'Mum, I've got exams next month. I'm revising all weekend.' I left my phone number and happily departed, wishing Christopher would take a leaf out of Nicholas's book. It was Saturday when the phone rang and it was my hostess's eldest daughter, who had a flat in London, informing her mother that Annie had come up for an exeat and had asked her permission to go out with a boy called Nick, and was this all right as she did not know the boy. My hostess agreed, with the condition that she must be in by eleven, which I thought was more than generous. In fact, I was livid, for I realised this must have been prearranged and that he had purposely not mentioned it to me. I rang the little monkey.

The lodger answered the phone. 'I'm so glad you've rung Sally. Nick went out after lunch and hasn't returned – is he playing rugger this afternoon?'

'No.' I hesitated and then decided to tell him that he was with his girlfriend, but not to tell him that I knew. 'Don't worry, they've probably gone to a film. He's very naughty not telling you or leaving a note. I'll be back tomorrow and deal with him then.' The next day another phone call came through, to say that Annie did not return till six that morning and by the time I arrived home I was beyond being calmed by the excuses of puberty. I was totally enraged by his unforgivable behaviour. I checked my anger as I entered his room, where he was hunched over his studies.

'Hi, Mum, did you get the report done?' He looked so tired, but managed a cheerful smile.

'Yes, thanks, and how was your weekend?'

'Oh, fine thanks.'

'Get lots of revision done?'

'Yup, fair amount.'

'Go out at all?'

'Mmm – needed a break from the work,' he said casually, looking at his books.

I knew then that he was not going to come clean, that in fact he wasn't intending to tell me anything. For an instant, I felt sorry for the lad – what bad luck for him I had been staying with Annie's mother.

'Nick, I rang the lodger yesterday afternoon and he was worried. He didn't know where you were or when you'd be back.'

He played it cool. He looked me straight in the eyes and replied, 'I'm sorry. I should have left a note. I joined up with a few friends.'

173

'So when did you come in?'

'About nine thirty, ten – I didn't look at my watch.'

'You were home last night by ten?'

'Oh yes, I know that's my bedtime.' Time for the coup de grâce.

'And what is Annie's bedtime?' He stared at me unflinching, like a waxed model at Madame Tussaud's. Not a muscle moved or twitched, but I could almost hear the turmoil in his brain. How could I have possibly known? How much did I know? How much should he tell me? Was it an intuitive guess? How could I have possibly known unless I had a private detective following him? The time lingered lightly for me, but heavily for him.

'Perhaps you didn't hear the question. I'm so sorry. I'll speak up. What is Annie's bedtime?'

Without moving his lips, he hissed through his teeth, 'How should I know?' He was still frozen to the spot and I held his eyes.

'You obviously didn't, if she didn't get home till six this morning.' He bit his lip and flicked back his hair, but said nothing. He knew he was at a disadvantage, not knowing how much I knew, and he was bright enough to realise that by opening his mouth he could well incriminate himself. Meanwhile, I was working out my next move. A shouting match with Nick would only create acrimony, and what I needed was co-operation.

I sat down, showing my intention to stay. 'Not only did you worry the lodger, what do you think Annie's sister felt when she didn't come home last night? She didn't know whether to ring the police or her mother – she was out of her mind with worry. Did Annie stay here?' It was obviously easier for him to answer direct questions.

'Yes, we went out to dinner and came back here and watched videos. We forgot about the time and when I looked at my watch she'd missed the last tube.'

'But surely you could have rung and explained this to her sister?'

'I told Annie to do that, but she wouldn't do it. She said it was too late.' He had completely relaxed and was now looking utterly miserable and exhausted.

174

'So Annie was in charge and you couldn't override what you knew to be a wrong decision?' He shrugged his shoulders and did not reply, and then added,

'We watched videos all night and then I walked her to the tube station for the first tube this morning.'

'That was noble of you. The gentlemanly thing to do would have been to see her home last night.'

'I know, Mum, I do know.' There was a certain despair in his voice.

'Well, I've learnt a lesson, Nick, that I can't go away for the weekend unless I take you with me, and that will be a limitation on both of us. Meanwhile, I suggest you sit down there and write two apology letters, one to Annie's sister and another to her mother.' I went downstairs to prepare some supper. He was too miserable to eat his.

'I think I'm going to bed,' he volunteered. As he was about to close the door I called him back. He popped his head round, leaving his body in the hall. 'Yes?'

'Just thought I ought to tell you. You're not getting a condom allowance.' I grinned, and for the first time that evening, he chuckled. Oh God, preserve us from growing up I thought, and wondered how well I would cope with ten bright sixteen-to-eighteen-year-olds from Beckenbrough.

Chapter 19

I had taken the bus to the dentist as my car had a flat battery. I leapt from the public transport and proceeded to climb down two dozen steps up to the base of a high-rise block of flats where the surgery was tightly crammed in between the ground floor flats. As I ascended, something alive was descending. At first glimpse I thought she was drunk. Her movements seemed unco-ordinated and violent as she pulled behind her a shopping bag. She was clothed in rags upon cast-off, unpatched rags. Her tiny, birdlike head, nose streaming, jerked from within a makeshift scarf, the little tendrils of broken veins jutting out under her thin, ageing skin. I lingered and looked at this moving bundle, who was having difficulties in controlling her trolley-bag. It was too big for her to lift down the steps and she was too frail to stop it pulling her down.

I approached her with one arm outstretched to restrain the speeding bag. 'Please let me help you, I'll carry it to the bottom.' My sentence was drowned in a shrill scream, outside the normal voice range. I was quite overwhelmed by the noise and horrified by the contortion on her face as she bellowed and bellowed in fear that I was about to rob her of her trolley-bag. I placed a reassuring hand upon her arm, but her screaming was unstoppable. I became frightened and looked quickly around to see if anyone was watching.

I felt like a criminal as I began to run up the rest of the stairs. I reached a dingy corner in the hallway and shook and chattered with fear. All I had wanted to do was help her. What is this world coming to when an old lady is terrified by an act of kindness? I trembled all over, no longer from fear but the brutal realisation that though I did not like this world we live in, I was still part of it. I had accepted disillusionment.

A few days later the doorbell rang. A young man, immaculately dressed in a grey suit, smiled at me in recognition. 'Hello Sal. How are you?' I delved back into the past. 'Don't remember me, do you?'

'I'm afraid not, but you're most welcome, come in and have a coffee.' He threw back his head and laughed raucously.

'You ain't changed have you? Don't know who I am and yet invite me in for a coffee – bloody typical. I'm Jason. The kid who you took in when my mother wouldn't have me.' I clasped him by the hand with both mine, but we both knew that was not enough and threw our arms round one another. 'The Prodigal Son returns,' he whispered in my ear as we embraced. As I made him a coffee he remarked, 'Blooming quiet here, where are the kids?'

'There are no kids here any more, Jason. Spark as you knew it, is closed.'

'Ah, no, that's terrible. I don't believe it. It can't be.' He shook his head sadly. 'Do you know, Sal, the best two years of my life were spent here and I bet you there are hundreds of kids who could say that.' I felt tears brim to the surface in gratitude, so quickly changed the subject.

'And what of you, Jason?'

'Me, Sal, well thanks to you teaching me to read and write, I've got a good job in insurance and I've got a nipper aged three months and I'm marrying the mum next week. Actually that's why I came round – to ask you if you'll come to our wedding.'

'Oh, Jason, I would regard it as a great privilege to be present at your wedding. Thank you.' We reminisced for an hour and I told him of my fight to keep Spark.

'What I don't understand,' he said, 'is that you don't seem

178

too depressed. Spark was everything to you. You lived and breathed it.'

'Yes, I did, didn't I? I have been very depressed, even bitter, but I think I've come through it. I see a new beginning for Spark, therefore a new beginning for me.'

'You've never doubted, have you? You were always strong.' I felt my soul turn inside me and a voice echoing up from its very depths that reached my throat in a tremble.

'No, Jason, you're quite wrong there. I was and am riddled with doubt, but fortunately or unfortunately I'm also riddled with faith in a God who knows better.'

As I lay in my hospital bed with all these memories engulfing me in waves of nostalgia, was I not making a mockery of those final words I had spoken with such conviction to Jason? If I had faith in a God who knows better, why was I so frightened of death? By deliberately plucking at the glorious past, was I not trying to escape my fear of the future? If I had faith, why did I not accept this illness that was devouring me? Was life really so precious to me?

Gradually I began to feel distanced from life, memory became like a gleaming star, a masterpiece of shining pictures of past and present joined together and fused in my mind. Seriously ill as I was, I drifted back into unconsciousness. Released from the burden of my body, I soared freely through space, separate from creation, from the fiction of life, hurtling towards that temperate season of non-existence. I found the thought of death quite soothing. But then the thought of the after-life quite fatigued me; after all, I had not adjusted too well to the world I left behind.

I saw a shaft of light. It revealed a mirror. I stared into it. My reflection was larger and stronger than my real self. As I stepped back, this aged shadow of self stepped with me and continued to follow me down the corridors of oblivion. Death no longer comforted me. I fled from the labyrinthine depths of eternity, relentlessly pursued, slipping and sliding, striving to escape the clinging, contagious darkness of that abyss that moments before was beckoning my spirit.

'I think she's coming round.' The indistinct sound pierced the misty recesses of my mind as I played hide and seek

179

with my senses. I desperately sought a shaft of light to find the mirror again. I wanted to reassure myself of that larger and stronger reflection that had now suddenly merged as a friend into self, for the shadow understood better than I did what remained for me to do, as it propelled me towards the twilight.

Then I awoke to a perfectly familiar world of whitewashed walls, the smell of bygone illnesses, the blue-uniformed sister bending from her military-like eminence over me, red and yellow and pink and purple flowers radiant in the sunbaked room.

'You'll live.' I recognised the agreeable, unsympathetic voice of my youngest son. Everywhere was peace and stillness. I hardly dared inhale the air. 'Course she will. She's got to raise half a million for Spark, ain't she?' the rasping cheerful voice of Freddy replied.

'When a man has had a great deal given to him, a great deal will be demanded of him,' said the shadowed voice from within. I had come back into the old world, into reality, to seek the elusive truth of my spirit. And to see Project Spark continue its work with the young, I am destined to remain on the front line.